9.60

# THE COMIC NOVELS OF CHARLES SOREL

# FRENCH FORUM MONOGRAPHS

## 32

*Editors* R.C. LA CHARITÉ and V.A. LA CHARITÉ

For complete listing, see page 146

# THE COMIC NOVELS OF CHARLES SOREL
## A STUDY OF STRUCTURE, CHARACTERIZATION AND DISGUISE

by
ANDREW G. SUOZZO, JR.

FRENCH FORUM, PUBLISHERS
LEXINGTON, KENTUCKY

To my parents

# ACKNOWLEDGEMENTS

Grateful acknowledgement is made to Joy H. Potter and A. Donald Sellstrom for their careful readings of this text, helpful suggestions, and encouragement. Thanks are also due to the University of Texas at Austin for subsidizing my research in Paris during the summer of 1978.

# TABLE OF CONTENTS

# INTRODUCTION

Charles Sorel's numerous works—both acknowledged and attributed—make of him one of the more prolific and diverse authors of his time. During his long life (1602-1674), he wrote treatises on Christian piety and games, histories, an encyclopedia, critical bibliographies, stories, and novels, ranging from the comic to the philosophic. Recently, after a long hiatus, his comic novels, the *Histoire comique de Francion*,[1] *Le Berger extravagant*[2] (or *L'Anti-roman* as of 1633), and, to a lesser degree, *Polyandre, histoire comique*,[3] have attracted considerable interest in critical circles. This new appreciation for these works has led to a long overdue reappraisal of Sorel's hitherto neglected importance as a major seventeenth-century author.

The grouping of the *Francion*, the *Berger*, and the *Polyandre* is by no means arbitrary, for Sorel himself placed all three together under the heading of the "comic novel" in discussions of that subgenre in *La Bibliothèque françoise*.[4] In so doing, he recognized a program common to all of them: a general censure of human failings, and, more importantly, the censure of literary abuses, which, in his view, were propagated by the novels of the time. In fact, it becomes apparent from his critical bibliographies and a reading of the comic novels themselves that Sorel's most enduring concern was the reform of literature which required as a first step the destruction of the contemporary novel. Paradoxically, he chose to accomplish this task by using an offshoot of that genre.

In his writings, Sorel shows that he was aware both of his historical antecedents and his targets. He saw the *Francion* as flowing from the Spanish picaresque tradition but nonetheless superior to it by the very choice of its protagonist. The Spanish "Livres Comiques ne sont que des vies de Gueux et de Faquins," whereas the *Francion* is "le Recit de la vie d'un Gentilhomme, qui veritablement estoit dans la desbauche, mais que parmi cela il monstroit beaucoup de marques d'esprit et de générosité" (BF, 59). Likewise, he admits to finding inspiration in *Don Quixote* for the *Berger*, but once again, his own work represents a greater achievement of the imagination, for it was "plus difficile de faire trouver des avantures agreables, pour un Berger qui ne pense qu'à son troupeau, que pour un Chevalier errant, comme Dom Quichot" (BF, 59). He also underscores the polemical slant of the comic novel—in this case, the failings of the pastoral—in his remarks on the *Anti-Roman* whose main character "n'a de l'extravagance que pour se moquer de ces autres Bergers et de tous les personnages de nos Romans."[5] Further, in his general reflections on the dangers which the reading of novels offers to the young, Sorel condemns the novel of courtly romance and adventure ("le roman de chevalerie") not only because its reading exerts a harmful influence on their studies but also because "elle les destourne encore de faire choix de quelque profession utile, leur faisant croire que la plus belle vie est celle des Chevaliers Errans" (CBL, 96). In short, the comic novel emerges not as an isolated phenomenon but originally as an outgrowth of a particular literary tradition, the picaresque, and simultaneously as a reaction against others, most notably the pastoral and knightly adventure novels. But the comic novel was not entirely negative: in condemning the abuses of contemporary novels, it opened the way for a more "realistic" form of narration, and a more "modern" form of literature.

The struggle to distinguish between illusion and reality establishes itself from the very first pages of the *Francion* as the dominant theme of Sorel's comic novels, and this struggle reasserts itself perversely in the *Berger* and more characteristically in the *Polyandre*. Accordingly, the term "illusion game" will be used to indicate this constant play on appearances which animates these works.[6] Sorel was preoccupied, if not obsessed, by the theme of deception. He felt that a preference for falsehood was endemic to humanity:

> Ce n'est pas d'aujourd'hui que le Mensonge se fait escouter dans le Monde, & qu'il y est mesme plus estimé que la verité. Son origine est aussi ancienne que celle des Hommes, à cause que naturellement ils ayment le déguisement & la feinte. (CBL, 85)

Indeed, the social ambient of the seventeenth century with its duplicitous courtiers constantly involved in Machiavellian intrigues did little to allay Sorel's vision of social interreaction based on façade.[7] Real intentions were rarely revealed in a forthright manner. Never perhaps has an age been more conscious of the conflict between reality and appearance. Sorel himself was imbued with this radical opposition. Moreover, as author of *La Maison des jeux*,[8] he also exhibited a highly developed sense of play evident in his fascination with games, from the simplest to the most complex. This keen enthusiasm for games, allied to an acute awareness of the conflict between *être* and *paraître*, orchestrates the comic novels, which are precisely extended exercises in accurate perception in a society based on ruse and treachery.

The illusion game postulates only one really important social exchange: the relationship between dupe and trickster. The object of this game from the characters' perspective is to prove one's lucidity and to enhance one's social standing. But, on a broader plane, Sorel uses the illusion game to satirize society and literature, to debunk both, and to create works of demystification. In short, he is a realist because he seeks at every turn to reveal hidden social motives and to unmask the conventions of literary deception accepted by author and reader alike. He knows that literature is built upon lies and feels that it therefore merits rejection. In a sense, through his comic novels Sorel has already partially foreshadowed the goals of Scarron and Furetière, though not as concisely.[9] Let us very briefly consider the three comic novels to obtain an overview of the workings of the illusion game.

The opening of the *Francion* is a beginning from almost total blindness suggested by nightfall, Valentin without his habitually worn glasses, his descent into the moat, the confusion of identities between the hero and a robber, Francion's failure as a *trompeur trompé* in his quest for Laurette, and, worse, his misunderstanding of her "love" for him.[10] The whole movement of the novel, thanks to its dramatic opening, becomes one of progress from ignorance and illusion to a clear, nearly cynical understanding of the world. Only the cheerful tone checks a potentially corrosive scepticism. Briefly, the deceived Francion reclaims his role as hero by recounting his youth to Raymond. This extended flashback shows that even from infancy he was particularly lucid —in that case, vis-à-vis superstitious servants who mistook a monkey for an other-worldly apparition. Later, he is presented outwitting his foolish and pedantic schoolmaster, Hortensius. Finally, he emerges from temporary student poverty with an understanding of the value of appearances, and he begins his apprenticeship in love. The only stumbling block to his perfection as an accomplished manipulator lies in his mistaking the prostitute Laurette for a worthy object of his affections. Agathe's account of her protégée's past and the subjective communication of the dream, which concludes by linking Agathe and Laurette, reveal the true nature of Laurette, his cunning adversary.[11] After the orgy, Francion moves towards a complete mastery of all sexual encounters and crowns his adventures by marriage to the beautiful Nays. Even she undergoes an unsought enlightenment which apprises her of his infidelities and insures perceptual parity between hero and heroine. The illusion game remains constant to the end of the novel, whether it be in the ruses of Francion's rivals or in his own against enemies, friends, and even Nays herself. All movement is determined according to a constantly varied dialectic based on a confrontation of dupe and trickster. This general orientation imposes a structural arrangement which leads to enlightenment and social success.

In the *Francion*, Sorel's illusion game emphasizes personal enlightenment in a corrupt society. Although he satirizes literary personnages and trends in that novel,[12] Sorel used the *Berger* for his most massive onslaught against literature. Once again the dupe/trickster relationship is dominant: Louis-Lysis falls into the hands of Anselme in Book I, and, for the duration of the novel, i.e., until his eleventh-hour cure, he and his servant Carmelin play the fools, to the enormous amusement of a group of gentry. The game as a quest for lucidity no longer exists. The multiplicity of dupes so common in the *Francion* disappears. Instead, with only one principal dupe, the novel focuses on his captivity to illusion—an enslavement which is inexorably exploited until every aspect of the contemporary pastoral is bludgeoned to death. Although the diversity of the illusion game is diminished in the *Berger*, its orchestrating power stands. Each episode serves as an amplification of Lysis' follies. But his follies always refer to some aspect of a literary genre. With this in mind, literature may be seen as a trickster and the readers who enjoy it as its dupes. Each of Lysis' extravagances, so unscrupulously encouraged by his "admirers," comprises yet another condemnation of the pitfalls of fiction. It is thus the reader rather than the principal character who is the apprentice in lucidity and the victim of a sardonic and teasing author.

In the *Polyandre* the multiplicity of dupes is renewed, but one key factor inhibits the verve of the intrigue: Polyandre, unlike Francion, never makes an error. He does deceive and maneuver quite deftly in his own interest, but his social omniscience and his rather staid maturity rob the novel of brio. Whether Sorel had planned any surprises or setbacks for him remains a matter of speculation. There are several dupes in the *Polyandre*, most notably Gastrimargue, who is somewhat reminiscent of Hortensius in the *Francion*. For him, as for the pedant, there is no struggle to overcome ignorance, no eventual enlightenment. The major game strategy seems to be, as in the *Francion*, the hero's eventual marriage with the young widow Aurélie. The dialectic of dupe/trickster again governs every move. At the same time, literature is attacked in the persons of the monomaniacs, most especially Musigène and Orilan. But the novel's mutliple objectives—for this is a novel of mores—never fuse due to its incompletion. It remains a melange of social and literary satire illustrated through various forms of duplicity.

As we have indicated, Sorel repeatedly stressed his enmity towards the contemporary novel and his preference for history over fiction.[13] Superficially, his vast literary output and the comic novels in particular contradict his ideological stance.[14] Yet a closer view of his comic novels corrects this apparent contradiction. Their tendency to debunk, to reveal hidden truth by dint of the illusion game differentiates them from the courtly and pastoral novels of the period and, at least for Sorel, links them to history through their passion for the truth, their realism:

Les bons Romans Comiques & Satyriques semblent plûtost estre des images de l'Histoire que tous les autres; Les actions communes de la Vie estans leur objet, il est plus facile d'y rencontrer de la Vérité. Pource qu'on voit plus d'hommes dans l'erreur & dans la sottise, qu'il y en a de portez à la sagesse, il s'en trouve parmi eux plus d'occasions de raillerie, & leurs defauts ne produisent que la Satyre. (BF, 57)

In short, Sorel's notion of a realistic portrayal is negative and, by implication, didactic. Realism is the lucid gaze of a somewhat cruel observer savoring human folly—the trickster. To understand this notion of realism, one must keep in mind the dialectical relationship of the comic novel with its courtly and pastoral counterparts; the comic novel, or anti-novel, is precisely a reaction to the idealized world of the other two. The grotesque, highly stereotyped characters which people it are often reproaches to the passionate knights and shepherds of the two opposing genres. If such comic characters hardly appear realistic today, it should be remembered that their realism often resides in the deflationary effect they have on other characters in other novels. Their realism is entirely intertextual; they are elaborations of an anti-literature consecrated to the destruction of the preposterous fiction that was the mainstay of contemporary readers. In that case, the comic novel's intricate, often scabrous illusion games which lay bare the deficiencies of human nature are impassioned protests against hackneyed literary conventions of obfuscation and occultation used to exalt the heroes and heroines of novels. Indeed, for such literary targets, the illusion game is meant to be a *jeu mortel*.

Such is the general outline of the workings of the illusion game and its relationship to realism in Sorel's comic novels. This play of appearances orchestrates the relationships between characters and the overall plot developments in each novel. The illusion game, both leitmotiv and plot structuring device, will serve as the framework for the analysis of Sorel's comic novels under the headings of structure, characterization, and disguise.

*Chapter I*

# STRUCTURE

The very suggestion that the seventeenth-century comic novel—whether Sorel's or others'—contains anything more than the most rudimentary structure will surely appear to many as a perverse and irritating anachronism. In all justice, one may object that Sorel's comic novels seem very random and unfocused in their arrangement, that the *Francion*, in particular, is at best picaresque in its format, and that it and the other two are clumsy agglomerations of repetitive tales. In fact, Henri Coulet forcefully expresses this viewpoint in his negative assessment of the *Francion* which he condemns as a "tissu informe de gauloiseries, de choses vues, d'aventures romanesques, de souvenirs littéraires et de contes satiriques dont l'ensemble est si indigeste."[1] Such observations reflect our own literary prejudices and tend to ignore or discount certain ordering principles which are constantly in evidence and were probably taken for granted during the period. A demonstration of such principles would perforce shed light on Sorel's work and on the literature of the time as a whole.

Any discussion of the elements of coherence or structure is necessarily subjective. Various factors will inevitably seize the attention of different critics. Indeed, despite the rather unreceptive attitude towards structure in the comic novel, some critics have already tried to point out various unifying aspects of the *Francion* and the *Berger*. Felix Freudmann pictured the former novel as a movement away from obscenity towards the ideal, personified by Nays.[2] Wolfgang Leiner has studied the famous dream sequence as an aspect of the internal cohesion of the *Francion*.[3] Jean Serroy and I have tried, from different perspectives, to justify the addition of the twelfth book in the 1633 edition. Serroy presents it as a baroque resolution to the problem of Francion's promiscuity, as the acceptance of finality in profusion,[4] while I view it as a means to achieve intellectual and (im)moral parity between the hero and heroine, as the "Book of Nays."[5] Fausta Garavini has shown, among other things, the intellectual coherence of the work throughout its successive additions and editions.[6] Most recently Jean Alter has studied the unity of narrative voice in the novel.[7]

The literature on the *Berger* is by and large quite recent. Structural commentary is relatively available, especially if one takes the *Berger* within its wider context as the *Anti-roman*. Elizabeth Tilton suggests that the novel is constructed like a legal presentation which carefully follows the format prescribed by classical rhetoric: Book I corresponds to the *exordium* and *narratio*; the entire fiction serves as a *confirmatio*; the "Remarques" form Sorel's *reprehensio*; and the debate in the next-to-the-last Book together with Lysis' conversion in the end make up a concluding summary or *peroratio*.[8] Caren Greenberg studies the thematic consistency of the work and demonstrates the elaborate reiteration of certain processes.[9] Daniel Chouinard views the intrigue and the following "Remarques" as antithetical but complimentary structures aimed at creating a "brouillage du discours."[10] One may also take a larger view, as Anna Lia Franchetti does, and see the *Anti-roman* as one particularly subtle stage in the unfolding of an ideologically coherent opus—as part of an intellectual development which parallels Sorel's summa, *La Science universelle*.[11] It becomes his critique on the problems of literature, just as *La Science universelle* addresses itself to the errors of philosophers.

The focus of this study will be more stylistic, addressing itself to two aspects of Sorel's writings that have particularly struck me: the use of "repetitive" episodes whose slight variations signal important developments in the plot and in the overall orchestration of the novels, and the use of antithesis to create long-range thematic interrelationships between characters and episodes.

Curiously enough, Sorel would seem to agree with those critics who reject structure in his work. With his customary polemic flair, he lambastes the novelists of his time and possibly himself as well:

> Ils entassent avanture sur avanture; il ne leur importe si l'on les trouve regulieres, pourveu qu'elles suffisent à remplir plusieurs Volumes; Aussi establissent-ils la beauté de leur Histoire à tout bouleverser, mettant au commencement ce qui devroit estre à la fin, & broüillant tellement toutes choses qu'on a peine d'en comprendre la suite; Si bien que ce qu'ils ne peuvent obtenir de la justesse de leurs incidens, ils pretendent de le gagner par la bigarrerie. . . . Il y a souvent de la multiplicité dans leurs evenemens sans y avoir de la diversité. (CBL, 111)

These harsh comments on the methods of his contemporaries—comments which should be read with extreme caution, always keeping in mind that Sorel was himself both an enemy and writer of novels—provide, even at their most damning, important information on the techniques of plot structuring and give evidence of Sorel's own awareness of the pitfalls of redundancy. Let us begin by assessing his initial reproaches—clumsy padding and confused plot structure—in the light of his own works as preliminaries to a discussion of repetition, or "multiplicité sans diversité."

It seems peculiar that the author of the *Berger* would criticize a padded intrigue. Indeed, that work is so lengthy that one is tempted to believe that its very size is a form of satire. In any case, whether it is a result of Sorel's caustic irony or of his polemic enthusiasm, lengthiness cannot be viewed as an inherent fault despite Sorel's comments. Brevity, in fact, rarely characterizes any of Sorel's work: whether explaining a game or writing a novel, he tends to be wordy. When writing novels, he turns out adventure after adventure with an *élan* equal to any of his contemporaries. Perhaps, in his usual spirit of overstatement,

Sorel was expressing his frustrations with the truly bad and all-too-numerous novels of the period rather than attacking the convention of endless adventures itself.

Sorel's attack on the esthetics of putting at the beginning what ought to come at the end does point out an important structural convention of the early seventeenth-century novel: the *in medias res* opening.[12] This convention automatically imposed a very contorted plot arrangement which relied on a flashback technique. Clearly, Sorel's *Francion* and *Polyandre* are, in part, a parody of this very composed "formlessness." The former begins with the castle adventure and then spends several books—almost the entire first edition—relating the hero's life up to the initial episode. Indeed, much of the strength of the intrigue derives from this format of exposition. The *Polyandre* starts with the teeming activity of La Foire Sainct Germain. During this bustle, Musigène has a portrait wrenched from his hands. This theft and the lives of several of the principal characters are explained retrospectively as the novel develops. Given this procedure, one can describe the opening of the *Polyandre* as a modification of the *in medias res* technique. The recognition of an organizing convention and the parodying of that convention already suggest a definite structural arrangement in two of Sorel's comic novels. In fact, the structure involved is not unlike that of a modern television crime series which begins with an act of extraordinary violence aimed at arresting the viewers' attention and then proceeds to move backwards and forwards in time until the resolution of the opening situation. Naturally, both the seventeenth-century novel and today's television series controvert the logic of historical narrative, but they do so to a very definite end: the esthetic pleasure of the reader/viewer. There is nothing random about the structure of either.

Despite his complaints about the general confusion resulting from this contorted narrative style, it should be kept in mind that Sorel praises *L'Astrée* in the same chapter of *De la connoissance des bons livres*.[13] Anyone familiar with D'Urfé's work knows that it contains enough peripheral intrigue to lose even the most impassioned reader. Relatively speaking, despite their numerous digressions, Sorel's comic novels are infinitely less convoluted than D'Urfé's interminable pastoral. Once again, one is compelled to view Sorel's apparent denial of structure with scepticism and to ask what he really means by "broüillant telle- ment toutes choses qu'on a peine d'en comprendre la suite." Is he referring to the works of inept authors or is he denying order and structure in all novels?

By carefully considering Sorel's charge of a multiplicity with- out diversity of episodes, we may supply an answer to the above question. Superficially, this accusation seems to apply very well to Sorel's own work. Each of his comic novels contains an abun- dance of tales and adventures which are extraordinarily alike, often to the point of trying the patience of the modern reader. A cursory glance at them reveals a series of women very predicta- bly seduced, monomaniacs and madmen consistently duped, and heroes successfully extricated from various familiar dilemmas. Yet this type of repetition is surely not due to human failing. It is indicative of a cultural predilection in which redundancy is the norm. Thus one should approach Sorel's critique with extraordinary caution and bear in mind that Sorel not only praised the *Berger* in *La Bibliothèque françoise*, but he also sug- gested that it was superior to *Don Quixote* because it required more imagination to think up diverse adventures for a shepherd than for a knight (BF, 59).

The obvious implication of the above is that Sorel was using a different notion of repetition from our own because he was writing from within a context of culturally conditioned redun- dancy. Even if he found most novels guilty of his charge, it would be rash to apply Sorel's structural criticisms to his own comic novels, for while he condemns most others for their repe- tition, he freely praises *L'Astrée* and the *Berger*, works which would seem eminently guilty of this practice. Clearly, Sorel had a more refined sense of diversity than the modern reader.

Given the above considerations, one must pay very close attention to the episodes of Sorel's novels in order to discover the "diversity" of apparently redundant sequences. This diver- sity may reveal itself in the subtle development effected in a character or theme through a slight alteration in the format of an apparently repetitious episode, or through the very positioning of such an episode, which may serve as a cue to a new development. A close reading should demonstrate that Sorel's comic novels reflect a cultural orientation in their "repetitious" episodes rather than an unconscious stupidity or literary ineptness, that their superficial redundancy belies a hidden, complex diversity totally dependent upon slight modifications occurring from episode to episode.

The structural significance of "repetitious" episodes can be illustrated by a study of examples from all three novels. The minor love affairs of the *Francion* clearly show how significant developments can be indicated within redundancy. Numerous and quite similar in construction, the minor love affairs superficially substantiate Sorel's own charge of multiplicity without diversity. Briefly, these episodes comprise the courtship of Diane, the seductions of Luce and Fleurance, the conquest of Joconde, and the surprise failure with Emilie.[14] A brief inspection of these affairs indicates that all of them play on three common elements which contribute to their repetitious nature: ritual communication in form of a love letter (*poulet*); the visual marks of a superior social station, i.e., the appropriate dress; and the deception of a guardian.[15] The Diane and Luce-Fleurance adventures occur before the libertine orgy, nearly the end of the first (1623) edition and the event which is generally conceded to be the novel's watershed. The Joconde and Emilie adventures form part of Francion's later Italian escapades.

The Diane adventure constitutes Francion's first essay at the art of courtship. A financial gift from his mother permits him to emerge from a loveless life of poverty and to purchase the appropriate fineries to court a woman. Diane is guarded by a vigilant father, and so Francion makes his first advances by a discreetly sent *poulet* which his rival expropriates. Through yet another letter, Francion finally proves his authorship and rises in Diane's esteem. Eventually, after a false alarm caused by her precipitous departure from the church of St. Séverin, he establishes himself as her exclusive suitor. Francion abruptly loses interest in her at this point. The game has ceased; even consummation is not required.

In the Luce-Fleurance seductions, a subtle variation is introduced. Francion is interested only in Luce's lady-in-waiting, Fleurance; Luce is his master Clérante's objective. Clérante, however, is not particularly intelligent, and so he prevails upon Francion to write a *poulet* to Luce—a *poulet* which is to pass as Clérante's own composition. Luce, like Diane, discovers the feint. In both incidents, quality will out, though in the first Francion clearly wanted his mistress to know the letter was his, while in the second he has every desire to conceal his authorship. Francion does eventually win Fleurance, but must "enjoy" the conquest of Luce as well. But we shall reserve commentary on these developments for our discussion on differentiation in ch. 2.[16] The essential point here is the creation of diversity by manipulating the effects of the *poulet*: variations on a theme.

In the original 1623 edition, the Diane and Luce-Fleurance episodes are followed by confessions of the hero's inability to give his attention entirely to any one woman.[17] In the latter confession, Francion complains of not being able to find a model of perfection, thereby justifying his inconstancy. This avowal might be viewed as a preparation for Nays, who will embody both beauty and intelligence and so provide a simplistic justification for the end of his errant ways. The statements following both episodes might also be interpreted as confessions of the impossibility of a perfect love relationship, and these two avowals might well be considered harbingers of the libertine promiscuity which Francion preaches at the orgy. In this case, even the commentaries which follow the Diane and Luce-Fleurance intrigues become part of a climactic development, more reinforcement than repetition.

But the essential structural function of these minor love affairs lies in the balance they provide to the hero's relationship with Laurette. By their very reiteration of the hero's successful sexual appeal and sublime skills in the rituals of courtship, they prevent the undermining of Francion's role as a manipulator and Lothario. Duped by a tart, he must and does present evidence of his erotic triumphs. Further, these minor affairs are related only after the scene involving Nays' portrait,[18] when

Francion's infatuation for Nays begins and his interest in Laurette starts to wane. They bear witness, therefore, to a developing strength as Francion turns to a new obsession. Because they end in the rapid abandonment of the women involved, they also prepare the way for the prompt dismissal of Laurette.

The next minor affair, the seduction of Joconde, occurs well after the orgy, at the beginning of Book X. The principal variant here is that for once the *paraître* is contravened. Francion is dressed in the guise of a peasant; he is working for Joconde's father as a gardener. In an off-hand remark to him, Joconde expresses her distaste at the lack of realism in pastorals. Francion then offers himself as proof of their verisimilitude by maintaining that he is a gentleman in shepherd's clothing. This is particularly mordant, as he has just emerged from a mock-pastoral "idyll" which proved that the peasants were nothing but superstitious dolts or sexual playthings. Again, the alert reader appreciates the subtle twist on a standard situation, the in-joke of Francion's successful seduction despite his lack of one of the key elements of courtship, namely, fine clothes. Otherwise, everything else is in order: the *poulet* is accompanied by a serenade and Joconde's parents are easily deceived. After attaining his ends, Francion remorselessly abandons Joconde with the facile self-justification that he must renew his interrupted quest for Nays.

The Emilie affair contains all the standard elements of the seduction intrigue. We can safely assume that Francion, leading a brilliant existence in Rome, is well dressed. He eventually manages to win the good will of Emilie's watchful mother, Lucinde; he also sends her beautiful daughter a discretely disguised love letter—a shepherd's lament. Just as he seems to be making great progress, Emilie, indignant over his dishonorable intentions, rejects him.[19] We learn all of this retrospectively in Francion's explanation to Raymond after he has been falsely accused of signing a marriage promise to the difficult Emilie. To make matters worse, Francion is later arrested on trumped-up charges of counterfeiting. Nays, disgusted on both accounts, temporarily repudiates him. In the light of these developments, the Emilie seduction goes far beyond bad luck in a foreign pecadillo. Instead, a superficially minor intrigue is linked to a kind of cosmic failure for the hero. A rather predictable success formula is suddenly reversed, and failure itself becomes the variation in the superficially monotonous minor love affairs. The Emilie affair thus assumes a special importance because it illustrates how breaking a pattern can have immense structural impact on the novel as a whole. Thanks to Francion's failure, Nays is delivered from marrying as a gullible lover and Book XII (the addition of the 1633 edition) is saved from the charges of being a boring and superfluous accretion. All of this requires some explanation.

Francion is not only a failure, but he is also the dupe of the seemingly innocent Emilie, who was in fact the agent of Francion's rival, Ergaste.[20] Emilie encourages Francion's advances only to have the pretext to accuse him of breaking a marriage promise and sink him both in public opinion and in Nays' eyes. The temporary success of that operation may be justified by the requirements of plot: a new and serious obstacle had to be invented to postpone Francion's marriage to Nays, keep up the suspense, and pad an additional book. But in terms of the internal consistency of the novel and the structure of Francion's development from the status of dupe to manipulator, an obvious question is raised: since Francion had mastered the game of illusion at the outcome of the Laurette adventure, since he had demonstrated increasing deftness in the manipulation of others, what structural inference must be drawn from this surprising relapse? Does it actually contradict or does it somehow reinforce the major movement of the novel from illusion to lucidity? Paradoxical as it may seem, both effects are realized, for deviation from the pattern of the hero's development is required to generalize that pattern. And furthermore, being extended to the heroine, the movement from illusion to lucidity thus encompasses the entire narrative. The apparently superfluous and repetitive Book XII turns out to have a critical function in the balance of the novel.

At the end of Book XII, the Nays intrigue had reached its terminal point; all obstacles to a happy marriage were removed, and the ceremony was announced. Only one factor was missing for a perfect resolution: while Francion had completed his education in lucidity, Nays still believed in his exclusive fidelity to her. It was, therefore, necessary to append a last book which would do for Nays what all the others had done for Francion, i.e., free her from illusion and teach her lucidity. But, whereas Francion's evolution moved him easily from confounding his original deceiver to conquering his ideal dupe, in the case of Nays the two antagonists were telescoped into one character, Francion, who had to play both roles. In other terms, Nays had to discover the true Francion, a philanderer—a relatively easy task despite his proclamations of love. But if Book XII were to parallel exactly the first eleven books, she would have to prove her newly won powers by casting a spell over Francion. It is the second part of that program which could not be carried out through a direct confrontation between Nays and Francion. Had she actually succeeded in mystifying him, the novel's resolution, which requires an equal lucidity on both parts, would be again postponed at the end of Book XII, for this time Francion would have to undergo the entire cycle once more. Since Nays would have to play in turn both the deceiver and the dupe, the resolution would become a perpetual seesaw between the two lovers, ever unable to meet as equally lucid partners. Such an ending, or rather the intimations of such an ending, would destroy the general movement of the novel and change its optimistic tone to one of deep skepticism.

The introduction of the Emilie episode provides an acceptable way out of the logical trap. On the one hand, through its open character, ending in the public hearings of the trial, it enlightens Nays about the real nature of Francion: although innocent of the marriage promise to Emilie, he nevertheless must admit his philandering. The important feature here is that this exposure does not involve Nays directly. She reaches lucidity, as it were, vicariously. The revelation is not a part of a specific and direct confrontation which brings a sudden reversal of roles or revenge. Francion, duped by Laurette, freed himself from illusion by a painful experience of truth, took his vengeance by taking Laurette, and cut loose from his deceiver. Nays, deceived by Francion, learns the truth at a distance through the experience of Emilie and need not strike back to prove her new lucidity. In fact, this vicarious discovery of truth leads naturally to a vicarious satisfaction of the second condition for the resolution of the novel. Substituting for Nays as concrete object of dupery, Emilie also substitutes as a concrete duper: by victimizing Francion through her own spell of illusions, she performs the function that the overall pattern of Book XII assigned to Nays. The latter, informed of the trick through the public trial, vicariously partakes in the role of duper, but again remains at a distance, innocent of any real contest with Francion. In short, the burden of the concrete implementation of the program is transferred from Nays to Emilie, but, by making public what normally would be a private affair, the benefits are transferred from Emilie to Nays. At the end of the episode, she equals Francion in lucidity, and yet she has not duped him herself; he does not have to retaliate; they finally become partners.

But what about Francion? Obviously, Book XII causes a setback in his amorous progress. And yet the structure of the novel is not really affected. Indeed, insofar as the polarity of illusion and lucidity is concerned, Francion's function reaches an end with Book XI. Book XII, in that sense, is not concerned with him, but with Nays. Thus, the repetition of the same structure in a second section with a second character has a much stronger impact as a reinforcement of the basic theme than the undermining effect of Francion's "relapse" in a section which no longer directly concerns him. Besides, the actual characters are not primarily involved; they serve as supports for the patterned unfolding of the illusion-lucidity game in all episodes. Each love affair, minor as well as major, pits the deceiver against the dupe. If the major affairs serve to organize the novel into two parts—Books I to XI following the progress of one character from illusion to lucidity, and Book XII doing the same for another—the coincidence of structures is here more important than the coincidence of identities. In that more general sense, the Emilie episode fulfills a capital function which confirms the parallelism of the two parts. Indeed, it stands at the beginning of Book XII just as the Laurette episode opens Book I: the curtain rises each time on a game of amorous dupery just as it falls in both cases on a lucid union. The two poles remain in a state of perpetual tension.

Thus, in their totality, the minor love affairs[21] of the *Francion* offer a series of parallel situations which demonstrate that courtship is highly ritualized; but, more importantly, they reinforce and even alter certain developments in the novel. They may be compared to baroque music in which a movement will suddenly resurrect itself in the same melody and rhythm, but in a different key. Despite their superficial similarity, they have varying structural functions. While the earlier intrigues counterbalanced Laurette's sway over Francion, the Joconde episode, as well as the Emilie misadventure, shows that, even during the quest for Nays, Francion has never really abandoned his libertine promiscuity. Finally, the Emilie fiasco saves the heroine from marrying as a dupe, forces her to abandon her own illusions about Francion, and makes their union one of disabused lucidity. Multiplicity thus does not exclude diversity; it is carefully nuanced in order that it may play a decisive role in the polar structure of the novel by insuring that both hero and heroine make the transition from star-gazing lovers to realistic, if not cynical, adults. These "redundant" tales are not the blunders of a feeble imagination, but rather they are elements in close interreaction which offer amusement through subtle variation.

Structure in the *Berger* poses less of a problem than in the *Francion*. Although there are many "digressive" tales intercalated among Lysis' adventures, all the episodes flow directly from one to the other; the locus of action remains relatively restricted, and the work appears more unified than the *Francion*, where the hero's adventures are spread out in space and time. The structure of the *Berger* is thus, at one level, fairly obvious: the constant amplification of Lysis' follies as he becomes more and more immersed in living the pastoral. Nevertheless, one finds occasional "repeated" episodes as well as thematic consistency and development in what may appear to be "unnecessary" plot expansions. Let us consider a few examples for the sake of argument.

A blatant case of repetition may be found in the slaughter of Lysis' flocks in Books I and XII respectively. In each case, Lysis shepherds a small group of mangy, valueless creatures. In both instances, he is brutally deprived of them and their loss elicits lachrymose apostrophes. In Book I, his cousin Adrian has the animals butchered; in Book XII, Bertrand, his landlord, has them sold for slaughter to pay the rent. The presence of Adrian, Lysis' guardian, on both occasions is significant. In Book I, Adrian tries to force Lysis to return to society. The slaughter of the flock represents a blunt attempt by his practical cousin to destroy Lysis' illusions. Adrian acts as the simple-minded agent of common sense with all the worst failings of such a mentality. He is an efficient but unidimensional character, the other extreme to Lysis and completely unattractive. He cannot offer an appealing alternative to the pastoral because his grasp on reality is also too limited, too conventional: for him everything is business. He can offer only a return to the petty preoccupations of the bourgeoisie, not a broader understanding of the world such as is later offered by Clarimond, the real spokesman for truth in the novel. In this context, the first slaughter represents a clumsy attempt to deliver Lysis from the world of illusion by another character who is himself incapable of understanding the complexities of the world. In fact, Adrian is sufficiently naïve to confide his charge to Anselme, who, despite his alleged intentions of setting Lysis back on the road to sanity, has no real interest in curing him. Rather, he wishes to convert the would-be shepherd into an object of amusement.

Although Adrian is not responsible for the liquidation of the second flock, the news of its slaughter occurs in Book XII almost simultaneously with Adrian's discovery of Lysis' hideaway, where the latter had fled to avoid his troublesome warden. It is important to note that Adrian has come to take Lysis back to Paris and the world of practical affairs. Adrian's efforts in Book XII also coincide with Lysis' last and most dramatic attempt to live the ultimate pastoral adventure by being "resurrected" from the dead through the intervention of Charite and also with the start of an aggressive push by Clarimond to put an end to Lysis' madness. Clarimond will, in fact, ally himself with Adrian against the other "shepherds." The slaughter of the flock, linked again with Adrian's clumsy efforts, reasserts the theme of the return to reality, at first aborted, but finally successful once a truly competent exponent of realism enters the intrigue. Clearly, the use of a "repetitious" event creates a certain balance between the opening and the latter portion of the novel, which suggests a long-range, rather subtle notion of structure by its very minute attention to detail.

While most episodes in the *Berger* do not really repeat each other, they are often not without affinities. The formats of Lysis' metamorphoses into maidservant, weeping willow, and finally classical hero provide examples of such interrelationships. All of these episodes are based on the willingness of other characters to humor Lysis and to feign belief in his various roles, which he takes completely seriously; all are united by the orchestrating presence of Hircan, "the magician," who is responsible for suggesting two of them. For every character but Lysis, they constitute a form of theater, plays to please a madman, and, as theater, they were already prepared by the Hôtel de Bourgogne episode, during which, taking a pastoral play for reality, Lysis actually intervened in the performance to the confusion of both actors and spectators. Interrelated, but conspicuously diverse, these theatrical episodes bring Lysis to his highest point of crazed exaltation just before his downfall.

But the interrelationship of episodes goes beyond a common thematic element like theatricality. Caren Greenberg discusses numerous, particularly complex structural processes which repeat themselves in diverse episodes. In fact, she adds a new dimension to the whole problem of repetition. In most cases, it is quite evident that one episode has very marked affinities with another. But Greenberg's work goes in the opposite direction: it indicates the hidden affinities. For instance, she points out analogous processes of dispersal in Anselme's discussion of the echo myths and Clarimond's "Banquet des Dieux." In the first instance, in the course of his argument with Lysis, Anselme demolishes classical lore by citing mutually exclusive variants on the echo myth. The end result of his reasoning is the elimination of any and all authoritative versions. In the second instance, the dissension of the gods leads eventually to their pulverization "like the body of Echo in the Daphnis and Chloe versions which Anselme cited."[22] The critic also elaborates on numerous other examples of such analogous processes: for instance, the transmutations of narcissism, which is first evoked in the echo argument, picked up again in Lysis-Amarylle's infatuation with his/her mirror image, and later articulated in Fontenay's tale. Elizabeth Tilton also discusses this repetition of motifs by different speakers as an analogue to *amplificatio*—the addition of adjectives.[23] Here, and especially in the examples cited by Greenberg, Sorel is consciously "repeating" himself, but with a new perspective: this time the reader must discover the similar elements in diverse episodes. It is as if the author chooses to demonstrate his powers in two radically opposed fashions: first, by comparing similar episodes which are, nevertheless, different because of important variations or functions contingent on their very similitude, and, second, by creating apparently divergent episodes which are, nevertheless, similar upon analysis.

With the *Polyandre* Sorel abandoned some of the more elaborate features of the *Berger*, most notably the appended remarks, and returned to a format much more similar to that of the *Francion*. But instead of a continuous misadventure which unfolds with linear regularity, the *Polyandre* offers a series of alternating adventures, many of which are recounted by the characters themselves. The main narrative line—Polyandre's pursuit of social advancement—is constantly punctuated, if not interrupted, by secondary tales, several of which are related by Polyandre himself. These digressions, quite repetitive in their portrayal of the characters involved, gradually create a past and thus depth for these characters, who are otherwise restricted to a very narrow time frame.[24] It would be presumptuous to draw ultimate structural conclusions about the function of these reiterative tales, since the novel remains incomplete. In fact, though the three tales of Gastrimargue and the two of Héliodore-Théophraste appear to be endless variations of the discomfiture of these monomaniacs, Sorel may even have objected that they were not repetitive, since they do cover a wide range of topics (from alchemy to marriage). In any case, in the *Polyandre* it is more the positioning of a repetitive episode than its variations which seems to count. In other words, just as the Diane and Luce-Fleurance tales in the *Francion* emphasize the hero's sexual worth after he has been hoodwinked by Laurette, the secondary tales of the *Polyandre* underline its hero's superiority in the pursuit of Aurélie by stressing his perspicacity and inventiveness. The position of the secondary tales of the *Polyandre* hints at a macro-structure within which they contribute to the overall unfolding of the intrigue.

One example of these integrated tales is Héliodore's story, recounted by Mélinte. Héliodore has already appeared in the novel as the elderly T(h)éophraste,[25] who, in an attempt to sell an interest in the philosopher's stone to Néophile, told him that to court Aurélie properly he would need to go to greater expense than a Roman emperor. Nevertheless, despite this zany intrusion into Néophile's love life, he remains a very undefined character until Mélinte tells his story to Clorinie's salon. At this point, Héliodore is invested with a checkered past as a charlatan who was reduced to a *trompeur trompé*. Thereupon follows a complete account of his current trickery in Paris, where he is still selling the philosopher's stone under the name of Théophraste. As usual, he has a stock of ridiculous hoaxes such as the Rosicrucian story to dupe the gullible, and also, as usual, he meets with very mixed success.

But what structural function can be attributed to this tale in an unfinished novel? For one thing, Polyandre has now begun to pursue Aurélie actively, although covertly. Néophile, her suitor up to this point, is in the process of being devalued: he is young, naïve, arrogant, and pretentious. Later, he admits to having been taken in by Théophraste, hence his perspicacity is downgraded. Similarly, the coquette Clorinie, who represents social pretension and hopeless vanity, has purchased beauty treatments from the charlatan at considerable cost. She prefers to believe that there are two Théophrastes in Paris, rather than admit that she has been duped. Her attitude also hammers home the point that society is an illusion game played largely by inept people. Polyandre is, by contrast, presented as an epitome of prudent judgment who acts only when all the facts are clear.

The tales about Gastrimargue, like those about Héliodore/Théophraste, seem also to have as one of their functions the seconding of the amorous quest of the hero. Polyandre himself recounts the last two stories about Gastrimargue and, through the telling of the first, wins approval of all the guests in Aurélie's salon, even of the difficult Phronyme, who tries to show that his talents are limited, but succeeds only in provoking the continuation of the story. Polyandre thereafter becomes the object of general admiration, a suitor whose cleverness makes him worthy of Aurélie. Later on, Polyandre tells the story of Gastrimargue's misfortunes in love to Aesculan, Néophile, and Musigène. This is an interesting and perhaps deliberately planned variation of the theme of Gastrimargue's woes, for Polyandre tells the carriage story at Aurélie's, while he recounts Gastrimargue's failure as a suitor to his two rivals for the hand of Aurélie. This can be read as a wry comment on their situation. Thus, Sorel may be using a change of subject matter in a relatively monotonous episode to convey a hidden message. In any case, one can be sure that, although the hero's life is never recounted in any of the tales, they have a distinct bearing on his situation in the novel. Perhaps Sorel was trying to achieve something more subtle than the digressions of the *Francion*, which, with the major exceptions of Agathe's stories, nearly always directly involve the main character.


   Up to this point, we have been concerned principally with the apparent "repetition" of so many episodes and situations, with the "clutter" of tales which seems to characterize Sorel's comic novels. In short, we have addressed ourselves to the problem of "multiplicity without diversity." Multiplicity, as we have seen, is not without diversity and thus is actually an important structuring element, not a fault. But this is not the only technique which Sorel uses to create interreaction between various segments of his comic novels, to give them a more solid structure. To be more precise, Sorel's comic novels rely extensively on polarities, on absolute and usually grotesque contrasts between characters, episodes, and themes. These contrasts constantly refer backwards and redirect attention to apparently random tales and events in the narrative.
   The *Francion* is developed on the basis of a global polarity of lucidity versus ignorance, the ability to discern between *être* and

*paraître.* As I mentioned earlier, its hero moves from amorous ignorance to a complete understanding of his relationship with Laurette and to an exercise of his perfected skills in the conquest of Nays. The latter likewise moves from an unquestioning adulation of Francion to an understanding of his philandering nature. Francion's relationship with the novel's monomaniacs is also based on polarities. Hortensius offers the most outstanding case. The exasperating pedant personifies everything the hero condemns: he is pretentious, ignorant, socially inept, baseborn, and verbose. His literary and social pretensions are constantly set off against Francion's real claims and abilities.[26] Hortensius' great ambition is to write a novel: he even boasts of his plans for a science fiction piece. Francion, on the contrary, although he announces that he will soon write the *Berger extravagant,*[27] has already expressed his disdain for authorship and his preference for anonymity.[28] In short, Hortensius is Francion's alter ego or his negative.[29] To a certain degree, the same applies to Collinet, whose courtly comments to various beautiful women suggest a grotesque parody of the many seduction scenes in the novel. In fact, even at the beginning of the novel, the perceptive and sensually vigorous Francion is contrasted with the credulous and impotent Valentin.

These character juxtapositions run throughout the novel, and they confer upon it a kind of playful, baroque inclusiveness, for they depict the ideal as constantly linked to its deformation, the two extremes of the human condition. This contrasting of character types can thus be described as a shorthand manner of depicting the entire human condition, which is summed up by a global antithesis rather than by a massive array of varied characters. In fact, these configurations of opposites follow Sorel's normal mode of argumentation: the articulation of extremes.

Perhaps even more striking than the juxtaposition of characters is the contrasting of entire episodes. A particularly dramatic example of this technique may be found in the relationship between the peasant marriage and the libertine orgy.[30] No critic has ignored this exceptional revel, and some have made it the focus of their attention.[31] It has never been suggested that the orgy might have a complementary relationship with another segment of the *Francion.* Yet there exist curious analogies between the libertine orgy and the peasant marriage, analogies which raise the question of whether the latter is not precisely the world of the orgy inverted, a grotesque "other" which sets off and confirms the views expressed during the libertine revel.[32]

Perhaps the most compelling reason for treating the peasant marriage as a mutilated version of the orgy lies in the ideology proclaimed during the latter. When Francion's statements are considered, it is clear that the peasant marriage represents everything he condemns. Francion dismisses marriage, uses Laurette to prove one can do very well without it, and calls for general promiscuity:

> Il vaudroit bien mieux que nous fussions tous libres: l'on se joindroit sans se joindre avecque celle qui plairoit le plus, et lors que l'on en seroit las, il seroit permis de la quitter. Si s'estant donnée a vous, elle ne laissoit pas de prostituer son corps a quel-qu'autre, quand cela viendroit a vostre cognoissance, vous ne vous en offenceriez point, car les chimeres de l'honneur ne seroient point dans vostre cervelle. (F, 316)

By making promiscuity the ideal of the elite, Sorel needed only to locate marriage among the peasantry to link it forever with inferiority, ignorance, and servility.

There are several points of deformation which confirm this ideological bias.

Language comprises one area of sharp contrast between these two festivals. At the orgy, Francion reproaches his host, Count Raymond, for using obscenities and insists on the need for the creation of a new erotic vocabulary which would differentiate the elite from the peasantry: "Je desirerois que des hommes comme nous, parlassent d'une autre façon, pour se rendre differents du vulgaire, et qu'ils inventassent quelques noms mignards pour donner aux choses dont ils se plaisent si souvent a discourir" (F, 321). His call for a new erotic vocabulary which would free women from the burden of shame associated with their sexual mores indicates the uplifting power of the word, a thirst for distinction, and an incipient libertine *préciosité*.[33] All this is recommended so that "de cela l'on peut apprendre aussi que nous avons quelque chose de divin et de celeste, mais quant a eux [the peasants] ils sont terrestres et brutaux" (F, 322).

At the other end of the spectrum from this call for verbal elegance is the clumsy proposal of the *badault* who tries to turn the wedding festivities to his own advantage. His statement reads like an exemplum of the point Francion will make at the orgy. All the young peasant can do to win the heart of his intended is mutter—interspersed by a brief proposal—the monotonous and stupid refrain: "Eu! ma mere m'a parlé de vous" (F, 273). Likewise, the various reflections of the local biddies constitute another demonstration of verbal ineptitude, for their conversation is limited to banal, slangy observations on the want of food and other petty details. In fact, their venal outlook forms an exact opposite to the ideal of *générosité*—moral, intellectual, even financial—which identifies the elect of the *Francion*. Both of these banal enunciations represent the language of the "terrestres et brutaux," the precise opposite of the libertine elite's word artistry. Thus, Francion's desire for differentiation is given striking relief.

The peasant dance heralded by Clérante's buffoonery is an amusing episode for a disdainful Francion. On the other hand, the passage relating to the libertine dance, with its torches swaying in the breeze, is perhaps the most passionate scene in the entire novel:

Cét air cy que les Musiciens reprenoient sur leurs Luths, apres que Francion en avoit recité un couplet, ravit les esprits de toute l'assistance. . . . Tout ce qui estoit dans la salle souspiroit apres les charmes de la volupté, les flambeaux mesme agitez a ceste heure là par je ne sçay quel vent, sembloient haleter comme les hommes, et estre possedez de quelque passionné désir. Une douce furie s'estant emparée des ames, l'on fit jouer des sarabandes, que la pluspart danserent, en s'entremeslant confusément avec des postures toutes gentilles et toutes paillardes. (F, 320)

This alliance of elegance and passion characterized by the oxymoronic "douce furie" and the contrasting "toutes gentilles" and "toutes paillardes" save the libertine dance from the animal sexuality which pervades the peasant celebration. The description itself carries out Francion's ambition to remove vulgarity from sexuality.

Even one of the crudest scenes of the orgy—the veneration of the "cul"—exercises a counterposed function to an event occurring at the wedding. The veneration assumes a new level of meaning when one recalls the diarrhetic finale of the marriage feast when, feeling the effects of a laxative with which Francion has doctored the rice, the entire marriage party finds itself compelled to make desperate trips to the privy. Both episodes begin within the realm of scatology, but, while one follows a down-grading course, the other undergoes a comical uplift. The ample behind of the orgy is humorously metamorphosed when likened to the breasts. Hence, the *derrière*—regarded by the other revelers as profoundly revolting—is transformed by Raymond's visual analogy into an object of comic eroticism.[34] The final adoration of the "ass" with a reverent kiss from all its former detractors redeems the *derrière* from its excretory function and triumphantly includes it in a healthy, Rabelaisian celebration of the body. Of course, the diarrhetic distress of the marriage feast is profoundly anti-erotic. The degree and savagery of this symbolic attack on marriage can be gauged by the fact that it is even extended to the bride, who publicly soils herself on the dance floor. But what could be more appropriate than besmirching marriage in a humiliating flow of fecal matter shortly before its philosophical annihilation? Marriage is shown to be gross, animal and vile—literally excrement, the polar opposite of libertine epicureanism.

Clearly the contrast of marriage and orgy results in the apotheosis of the libertine credo while virulently airing class feeling. Francion's attitude towards the peasants permits them no nobility and precious little humanity; they are no more than buffoons to be manipulated at his pleasure.[35] But there is little point in reworking these observations in terms of class struggle. Social inequality was the order of the day; what is in question are the esthetic principles or needs of the novel, themselves a product of this social structure. The class prejudices expressed within the *Francion* should draw attention to an antipodal world view, one which is based on a division of persons and experiences into complementary segments of the desirable and its opposite—the deformed double. The orgy, when linked to the peasant marriage, completes a juxtaposition endemic to the baroque—the vertiginous coupling of two worlds which are curiously expressions of the same.

This form of dramatic antithesis illustrates how two apparently unrelated episodes are quite interdependent and how different sections of the *Francion* are coordinated. The peasant marriage is a flattering preparation for the orgy, and it must be read in juxtaposition with the latter, not as an isolated adventure.

In the *Berger*, polar relationships assert themselves more consistently and more emphatically. The distance between the pastoral ideal and brutal reality is relentlessly underlined: whether it be the shepherd Lysis addressing his mangy flock or the metamorphosed Lysis discharging his "sap" from the heights of a weeping willow. This juxtaposition is more frequently one of vision than one of action, for the contrast comes principally from Lysis' refusal to see the world as it is. Understandably, language plays an even greater role in these grotesqueries than elsewhere. For instance, the extravagant "histoires fabuleuses" of Polidor and Méliante which are set in Persia are followed by Carmelin's tale of his life beginning with the story of the tiny M. Taupin and his enormous wife Radigonde. Both Polidor's and Mélisante's tales contain comic elements of self-parody. Polidor's allusions to his lady love resume the theme of the literalization of metaphors initiated by the portrait of Charite.[36] Méliante's description of the castle siege and attendant events is so absurd that it undermines the heroic narrative.[37] But formally and stylistically, these tales are radically opposed to Carmelin's story, which is more appropriately termed picaresque, consciously lower-class in diction and verisimilar in its own curious way.[38] As Lysis predicted, the story becomes "une farce après une tragicomédie" (BE, 320). Significantly, Clarimond, Lysis' eventual savior from madness, announces his preference for Carmelin's story over the other tales (p. 329). His attitude may be seen as an argument for the comic novel in flattering contrast with opposing genres.

In the same vein as Carmelin's story, Clarimond's "Banquet des Dieux" offers a similar example of antithesis: it is a burlesque piece which ridicules mythology and operates in complete contrast to Lysis' own exalted understanding of mythology. Characters like Anselme also contribute to this linguistic (as well as perceptual) antithesis by speaking in a commonplace, commonsensical manner in reply to Lysis' tirades. Even nomenclature fulfills the same purpose: Lysis is really Louis, the bourgeois, and Charite is Catherine, the maidservant. In short, the novel weaves a network of grotesque juxtapositions which stress the theme of madness and hold the work together by binding tales and characters in opposing sets.

In the *Polyandre*, antithesis is largely confined to the hero versus the monomaniacs. The latter represent various social defects, a want of "mesure" (Gastrimargue, gluttony and pedantry; Musigène, the faults of "poetic" expression; Orilan, excess in love) and illustrate the incorrect way of making oneself a place in society. Polyandre, on the other hand, infallibly demonstrates his adroitness in all situations. He is also juxtaposed with Néophile: his prudence and success in pursuing his passions versus the latter's impetuosity and vanity. Nevertheless, the antitheses of the *Polyandre* remain more restrained than those of the preceding novels. One reason for this is perhaps the multiplication of monomaniacs in the *Polyandre*; there are too many singular characters to focus exclusively on a blatant contrast like that between Francion and Hortensius. Further, as shall be discussed in ch. 2, the monomaniacs of the *Polyandre* are not always entirely repulsive characters; their mixed traits make them less suitable for the kind of absolute contrasting so frequent in the *Berger* and the *Francion*.

Even if less prevalent in the *Polyandre* than in the two earlier novels, juxtaposition or antithesis may be said to play a structural role in the comic novel that is nearly as important as the "repetitive" episodes in the creation of unity. The very ubiquitousness of this technique creates a kind of stylistic coherence as well as thematic unity. The dynamic oppositions within Sorel's comic novels form part of the illusion game, for they are consistently articulated along the lines of trickster and dupe, the lucid and the blind.

In a curious way, antithesis echoes the classical manner of disquisition then in fashion: the argument is stated, its converse is offered, and finally a resolution is reached—one which basically favors the initial position. The use of antithesis suggests an inability to state one condition without immediately calling forth its radical opposite. It seems somewhat related to Genette's concept of baroque "alterity," a cultural imperative that embraces the world in inclusive opposition: the ideal immediately calls forth its deformation and vice versa. In both classical disquisition and the oppositions of the comic novel, nuance in the modern sense does not exist. Both move from one extreme to the other. Subtlety and diversity are found not in a given argument, character, or scene, but in the radical oppositions which occur within these and other entities, in the dizzying leap from one idea or condition to its absolute opposite.

Antithesis always implies a broad range, but tempers extremes by juxtaposing them. If the antitheses of the *Polyandre* and the *Francion* set their heroes advantageously apart, those of the *Berger* mark Lysis' insufficiencies. But in both cases, antithetical movement is generally aimed at the posture of society and literature, i.e., the overinflated ideals of the time. And so, while antithesis surely glorifies the protagonists of the *Francion* and the *Polyandre*, it also reflects a certain discomfort with the dominant value system: marriage appears undesirable, social status does not always coincide with the innate worth of the individual, and traditional literary forms are hollow. Antithesis thus not only juxtaposes, but it also exposes, and, by creating a sense of malaise about absolutes, favors realism.

This prominence given to antithesis in Sorel's comic novels marks them as stylistically very much part of their time. This trope may be found in abundance in every aspect of seventeenth-century literature. One need only refer to the "infiniment petit" and "infiniment grand" of Pascal's *Pensées* to call to mind but one outstanding example of this technique. Indeed, the conflict between *être* and *paraître* is itself the antithetical matrix which encloses both the comic novel and seventeenth-century literature as a whole. Thus, it is thoroughly in keeping with the culture of the times and logical that antithesis should serve as a cohesive technique which joins themes and characters, that it should function as a structuring element in what on the surface may be seen as a random series of tales composing Sorel's comic novels.

Elaborate contrasts and "repetitive" episodes often misperceived as digressions figure, then, as key elements in propelling plot development and in building macro-structures for these novels. All of these structuring devices operate within a framework of play. Sorel, with his vast knowledge of games, makes his novels into contests of perception in which victory goes to the most astute players. Inevitably, these contests beget structure, for there is no game without rules. The illusion game thus implements a naturally convoluted "baroque" format through its labyrinth of trickery which unfolds into patterns revealing refined analogies, subtle rhythm, and surprising balance. Indeed, there is more to Sorel's game than meets the eye.

*Chapter II*

# CHARACTERIZATION:
## HEROES AND ANTI-HERO,
## MONOMANIACS AND MADMAN

While Sorel's comic novels are peopled by hosts of diverse characters, only two compelling types emerge as dominant: heroes or manipulators of illusion and monomaniacs or victims of illusion.[1] These categories should be further expanded by adding "anti-hero" to the former, to cover the particular problems created by Lysis, protagonist of the *Berger*, and "madman" to the latter in the isolated, but important, case of Collinet, in the *Francion*, in order to consider the ambiguities which this particular character type creates. Nearly all of the relationships between Sorel's personae, even those of allies and lovers, are generated by the dynamic opposition of hero versus monomaniac, which is one of the key devices in the advocacy of "realism" and the destruction of the contemporary novel. This radical opposition between two classes of characters is, in fact, a logical development of the narratological technique of antithesis discussed in ch. 1. The discussion to follow will, to a certain degree, be an expansion of the antithetical aspects of structure and its polemical ramifications, but it is equally an examination of the evolution of specific types within Sorel's comic novels. And so this chapter will describe the body of traits which mark each individual character while demonstrating that each one is really a variation on a given theme rather than a discrete, human personality, for Sorelian characters are subordinate to the ideological development of the narrative and figure principally as emanations of propaganda in the advocacy of literary reform and general insight.

## A. Heroes and Anti-Hero

The use of a hero, despite the temporary eclipse of this practice in the *Berger*, remains essential to the *Francion* and the *Polyandre*, where the protagonists constantly stress the values of lucidity and perspicacity. Of key interest in the study of the hero is the deterioration of this ideal from its initial personification in Francion, its inversion in Lysis, and its unsuccessful restoration in Polyandre. In other words, an examination is required of the decline in that dramatic tension which was so marked in the struggles of the libertine Francion, and so absent in the impotent blindness of the crazed shepherd Lysis and in the bland self-assurance of the staid bourgeois Polyandre.

It should be noted that Sorel's ambivalence towards the novel, his withering sarcasm, and his generally disapproving attitude towards human affairs rendered his portrayal of the hero particularly problematic. Inevitably, his hero could not simply figure as a unidimensional champion of the good and the just. Elements of craft and calculation would necessarily form part of his character, for Sorel sought to repudiate the moral perfection of the knight and shepherd heroes of stock novels. In fact, Sorel's satirical objectives would even lead him to refuse to the protagonist of the *Berger* the very status of hero.

The names of Sorel's heroes are highly symbolic. Each conveys the message or key theme of the novel. "Francion" has a number of connotations, most notably "frank," "free," and "French" or "France." In other words, the name offers a winning combination of libertinism and nationalism. Sorel explains that Polyandre's name is from the Greek "voulant signifier un homme qui vaut autant que plusieurs autres, ou qui est propre à beaucoup de choses, & mesme à tout faire" (P, I, ã iii). For the two heroes, there is no opposition between name and function, but one can remark in their names a movement away from the youthful exuberance of the first towards a greater emphasis on social adaptability. On the other hand, the case of the anti-hero of the *Berger* is quite different. His double name, "Lysis-Louis," suggests the whole opposition between modern reality and the perverse attempt to recreate the world according to a pastoral image. It also links Lysis to Sorel's monomaniacs whose names usually have an ironic relationship to reality: Valentin, the patron of love; Hortensius, the great orator; Musigène, the child of the Muses.

While the struggle between illusion and reality remains a constant in all of Sorel's comic novels, its most forceful and vital representation from the standpoint of the hero occurs in the *Francion*, the novel of libertine apprenticeship. However clever and superior the young Francion may be, he is obviously flawed at the onset. Outwitted by the prostitute Laurette in the very first book of the novel, he must learn her nature, act upon this knowledge, and then move on to the conquest of his ideal dupe, the Roman beauty Nays.[2] The novel thus shows the hero in a position of learning and struggle. The amorous arena, although the widest, is, however, only one area of the conflict which engulfs a society infatuated with outward appearance. Francion must not only triumph in the erotic, but he must also outwit inferior masters, defend himself against a sadistic pedant, and deal with economic adversity. In this struggle, he clings to the precepts of his libertine philosophy, which he learns to conceal in all but the most select of milieux: that of the revelers at Raymond's castle. His very fallibility constitutes his principal appeal, and the numerous setbacks he encounters, including the disastrous interruption of his marriage plans in Book XII, make his adventures into a series of intellectual and dramatic dilemmas spiced with peripeteia.

In the *Berger*, Sorel completely inverted the notion of heroism by choosing as his main character an amiable maniac who had lost his wits from reading too many novels and poems. This choice made the *Berger* into a far more exclusive vehicle of literary satire than the *Francion*. In fact, Lysis' behavior becomes a point-by-point *reductio ad absurdam* of the most flagrant contemporary excesses in the pastoral and chivalric novels. While lucidity remains the dominant value in this exposition of follies, intellectual perspicacity is clearly banished from the mind of the principal character. Instead, Sorel situates this quality among the "antagonists," most notably Anselme, Hircan, and Clarimond, who eventually becomes the chief agent of Lysis' return to sanity. In the *Berger*, the protagonist as hero is discarded in favor of a protagonist with many affinities with the monomaniacs in order to serve the needs of Sorel's sweeping satire of literature.

Years later in the *Polyandre*, Sorel returned to the notion of the protagonist as hero, but he was unable to create a main character as fascinating as Francion. One of the chief problems in commenting on the nature of this hero lies in the fact that the *Polyandre* is unfinished, and we simply do not know the ultimate fate of its namesake, although we may well assume that it would have ended in Polyandre's marriage to Aurélie. But the depiction of Polyandre poses problems enough. Marked from the beginning by the epithet "adroict," Polyandre never requires any form of apprenticeship. Rather, as a mature bourgeois, he confronts the world with a calculating and omniscient eye which robs the intrigue of any excitement. He seems to be a Francion ten years older and set on a more modest course. Polyandre's longest anguish endures approximately one brief page: Aesculan tells him that he does not wish his son Néophile to marry Aurélie and thus raises Polyandre's hopes, only then to admit that he himself wishes to marry her. Instead of suffering a bitter and frustrating setback, Polyandre simply tells himself that he will be able to handle his master:

Toutefois il pensa que sans s'interesser beaucoup, il pourroit contenter ce vieil amant en des choses indifferentes, qui tiendroient son esprit dans l'attente de mieux. Voilà donc que par une adresse singuliere il a destourné les amours du fils de leur premier but, & qu'il conserve celles du Pere, ayant le secret d'estre le rival de l'un & de l'autre sans perdre leurs bonnes graces. (P, II, 256)

One never feels any doubt about the outcome. Lucidity and self-assurance are so allied in Polyandre that even peripeteia lose their savor. Polyandre, Francion grown old, is the paragon of bourgeois existence. Sorel consequently spares him Francion's failings, to the detriment of the novel.

Heroes in Love

Since all of Sorel's comic novels are to some degree parodies
of the grand passions celebrated in contemporary literature, it is
important to examine how each of his heroes and his anti-hero
react to love, and it is necessary to see how their successes or
failures are intimately tied to their lucidity or lack of that quality. In general, we must consider how the relationship of trickster and dupe functions in the affairs of the heart.

Characteristically, Francion is the most energetic of Sorel's
heroes. We meet him in his first dangerous misadventure, when,
after subduing the credulous Valentin, he attempts to scale the
wall to his mistress. Since I have sufficiently discussed this episode elsewhere,[3] I prefer to insist upon the terminology which
Francion uses to describe his initial infatuation with Laurette.
It is important because it shows a marked affinity with Lysis'
multiple descriptions of Charite, i.e., it is indicative of a complete misunderstanding of the nature of things. In fact, Laurette
is the object of a passion which can only be expressed by the
worst clichés, as Francion's words clearly reveal:

Aussi tost la fiebvre d'amour me prit avec une telle violence que je ne sçavois ce que
je faisois. Le cœur me battoit dedans le sein plus fort que cette petite roüe qui mar-
que les minutes dans les montres. Mes yeux estincelloient davantage que l'estoille de
Vesper; et comme s'ils eussent esté attirez par une chaisne a ceux de la beauté que
j'avois aperceuë, ils les suivoit tout par tout. La bourgeoise estoit mon Pole vers lequel
je me tournois sans cesse. (F, 94)

The exaggeration, the inclination towards the grotesque comparison—"cette petite roüe"—obviously undermine the supposed
nobility of Francion's passion and portray him as a prisoner of
hackneyed language. This particular passage is also part of a
flashback, and the reader already knows the true nature of Laurette. The contrast between the reality—the cunning prostitute—
and the ideal described by Francion illustrates the disjunctive
technique so characteristic of Sorel.

One need only recall that in Lysis' case Charite is a serving
girl, and yet the descriptions he gives of his beloved are consistently inappropriate. They are no more than a string of clichés:
her hair, "ces beaux fillets d'or qui parent sa teste, ces inevita-

bles rets, ces ameçons, ces apas & ces chaines," her cheeks are "parsemees de lys & de roses," her lips "font des branches de de corail," etc. (BE, 38). Again, the same process of emphasizing the disjunction between the lover's vision and reality is utilized for hero and anti-hero alike. In this instance, the only difference between Francion and Lysis is the degree of hyperbole in their respective effusions. The use of literary clichés immediately signals a failure of lucidity. In Lysis' case it points to a permanent failing, whereas with Francion this manner of expression marks an early stage in the eventual passage from blindness to true perception, the hallmark of the Sorelian hero.

In Francion's other adventures, he will treat most women as less than goddesses and thus express his maturation as a libertine. He reserves similar effusions for Nays alone—a trait which links Laurette and Nays and establishes a contrapuntal relationship between his two great passions: Laurette is the obstacle to be overcome, the great trial of Francion's lucidity, while Nays is the ultimate objective, namely, what Laurette was originally misperceived to be. But again, the use of literary effusion in Nays' case signals that there are once more many dangers in this amorous quest, not the least of which is the peril of clichéd thinking with its inevitable distortion of reality. After all, Francion and Nays' marriage will not be a triumph of passion, but one of pragmatism and mutually shared lucidity. It is natural, therefore, that a literary mind-set should be sarcastically signaled as inappropriate, for the hero may be dupe neither of himself nor of others.

Rather than dismissing the main character of the *Berger*, we should view Lysis as a kind of Francion in reverse: he works in opposition to the former's example by persistently obfuscating the simple matter of his passion for a serving girl with poetic folderol. Nevertheless, as has just been shown, there is a certain affinity between the satirical treatment of both Francion and Lysis: both are ridiculed when the objects of their passion are unworthy. In both cases, their goals are realized: Nays is the apt reward for Francion's growth, for the development of his perspicacity, while Catherine is the logical reward for Lysis' perversity. But even then he cannot marry her until he acknowledges the world as it is, not as he wants it to be. In the Sorelian order, lucidity must precede union for hero and anti-hero alike. Typically, however, characters must reap what they sow, and Lysis, following a trajectory which could be called the negative of Francion's, must accept an alliance with an inferior. By his willfulness, he sacrifices the advantages of great wealth and renders himself an unsuitable party for an equal, not to speak of a superior. Conversely, Francion marries advantageously: his bride is not only a woman of noble station, but an exotic foreigner to boot.

Polyandre, as I have remarked, moves rather assuredly towards his goal. The striking change in Polyandre's case is the diminution of passion, or, at least, of impassioned effusions. He warms to Aurélie, but initially refuses to do anything contrary to his master's interest. Yet, at Aesculan's behest, he distracts Néophile by calling his attention to Aurélie's younger cousin and effectively rids himself of the young man's rivalry. As already stated, even Aesculan's interest in wedding Aurélie causes only the briefest perturbation. Instead, Polyandre embarks on a campaign of calculated intellectual display to prove his superiority to his intended. His storytelling—the tale or, rather, tales of Gastrimargue—proves his excellent wit and wins the general approval of Aurélie's salon. The word, more than physical appearance, is one of the greatest differentiators in Sorel. Those who can wield it well, i.e., satirically, eventually have their way. Lysis' misuse of words indicates his derangement and assures his failure. The Sorelian hero, on the contrary, is never at a loss for the right expression; he is equally quick at understanding innuendos and at subtlely communicating his own thoughts. Language correctly employed is in itself a form of power.

A curiously common aspect of courtship in both the *Francion* and the *Polyandre* is a preference for a young widow—Nays or Aurélie—as the appropriate mate for the hero. Francion, for example, rejects Hortensius' observation that "les secondes noces n'avoient rien de meilleur que les viandes reschauffées" (F, 461) with an appreciation for a widow's experience and a reflection on his own promiscuity.[4] Aurélie, Polyandre's preference, is already a mature woman. Sorel's privileged place for widows as objects of his heroes' passions suggests a valorization of experience and a distaste for naïveté. He deliberately chooses a sexual initiate and thus establishes a certain parity among the couples. Francion is an avowed libertine of many adventures; Polyandre is too old to be without carnal knowledge and yet too discreet to brag about it. In a sense, widowhood is the convenient combination of *honnêteté* and experience. Without such a marriage option, the heroes would be condemned to marry either virgins or tarts. The rejection of the first option, the disdain for virginity, is at once a repudiation of literary convention and a valorization of carnal knowledge, a double rejection of illusion. Significantly, Lysis presumably takes a virgin for a bride; this clearly implies that the anti-hero could benefit from neither wisdom nor experience in his wife.

Thus, passion in Sorel's heroes is governed by the need for an equal, not a goddess to be adored, but someone who has fully tasted life. In the case of Polyandre, it is clear that there is an admiration for Aurélie's intelligence and social expertise. For Francion, the original notion of parity resides at the level of sexuality itself. But Sorel corrects this situation by making Nays his equal in lucidity in Book XII. All passions are played out under the rules of *être* and *paraître*, with both Polyandre and Francion showing their mastery of this game and eventually conquering their mistresses—most especially so Polyandre, whose mistress can appreciate his intellectual subtlety. Lysis, of course, demonstrates the laws of the game working backwards.

Passion is always undermined by sarcasm in the comic novels. Clearly, life viewed as a game of wits rules out effusions. The man who is always calculating may understand sensuous pleasure, but the contemporary language of passion, so hyperbolic and emphatic, is completely inappropriate to a consciousness that sees the world as ruse and feint. In fact, the world view of the comic novels makes it nearly impossible to speak of passion in Sorel. Rather, amorous pursuits are subsumed under the all-consuming illusion game; they are reduced to another aspect of social manipulation. Francion's effusions are canceled out by sarcasm, Lysis' by madness, and Polyandre is simply too staid to pant and sigh.

The Differentiation of the Hero

Besides recounting the amorous activities of his heroes, Sorel is also very much preoccupied with the process of differentiating them from a host of secondary characters, who, though allies, often unjustifiably enjoy a higher social station. With Lysis, the anti-hero, differentiation naturally works to the opposite end by constantly signaling his failings. The most outstanding examples of differentiation in the *Francion* are Raymond and Clérante. Relationships in the *Polyandre* exhibit a certain similarity to those in the *Francion*, especially in the cases of Aesculan and his son Néophile. In each novel, there must be a righting of social inferiority so that the natural superiority of the hero may assert itself. This is accomplished predominantly, though not exclusively, through erotic success.

Francion's relationship with Raymond is somewhat ambiguous. Raymond is a count and the mysterious gentleman who lends a sympathetic ear to the story of Francion's youthful adventures. Nevertheless, he is clearly marked as an inferior. Francion has accused him of theft, and this charge is never refuted. More importantly, the scope of Raymond's vision is demonstrated to be consistently deficient when compared to Francion's. In the discussion of erotic pleasure, Raymond sees no problem in enjoying a less-than-ideal partner, and he offers crudely pragmatic advice.[5] For Francion, however, reality may not be trifled with: the ideal must not be merely a figment of the imagination; it must be what it appears. Raymond figures as the exponent of a coarse and unenlightened sensuality. There are further indications that Francion's eroticism is of a higher order: at the orgy, he rebukes Raymond for his obscenities and calls for a new language of love. All the women approve his program and thus indicate that Francion has the true libertine vision, one that frees sensuality from shame. The text leaves no question that Francion's superiority as hero issues directly from his lucidity:

Chacun admira le bel et subtil argument de Francion, qui n'a guere son pareil au monde, n'en desplaise a tous les Logiciens, dont les esprits sont couverts de tenebres, au prix de celuy dont il estoit doüé. Les femmes principalement approuverent ses raisons, parce qu'elles eussent esté bien ayses qu'il y eut eu des mots nouveaux, pour exprimer les choses qu'elles aymoient le mieux, afin que laissant les anciens, qui suivant les fantaisies du commun ne sont pas honnestes en leur bouche, elles parlassent librement de tout, sans crainte d'en estre blâmées veu que la malice du monde n'auroit pas si tost rendu ce langage odieux. (F, 322)[6]

Likewise, in his relationship with Clérante, Francion is quick to set himself apart from his master. In the Luce adventure, Francion triumphs over Clérante both erotically and intellectually. Later on, during their stay in the country, Francion voices his distaste for the conversation of rustics—one of Clérante's favorite pastimes. When both go in disguise as musicians to the peasant marriage, Clérante has to play the cymbals, the only instrument he can manage, while Francion plays the violin. Francion's natural superiority is clearly incontestable.

Polyandre's dealings with Aesculan and Néophile are similar to Francion's relationships with his "superiors."[7] As previously shown, he outwits them both in sexual rivalry by distracting the one and holding the other in check. Curiously, his charge and master, Néophile, goes through a series of adventures which evoke the escapades of Francion. Early in the novel, Néophile mistakes a crazy old hag, Guérinette, for his mistress Aurélie, just as Francion takes an old wretch for a young serving girl and Agathe for Laurette at the end of the dream. Néophile reacts with similar exasperation; however, his bad temper gets the best of him and only Polyandre's intervention sets things aright. Néophile's brash immaturity serves as a foil to Polyandre's levelheadedness. Later on, Néophile engages in a series of adventures in disguise and even writes a promise of marriage to Nérine, which creates difficulties similar to those which Francion encountered from Emilie. Only his friend Géliaste's deceitful strategies save him from an undesired marriage.[8] However, Néophile's status is not enhanced by this maneuver. He is a blunderer who nearly got trapped. These episodes may indicate that an older Sorel wished to repudiate the youthful exuberance which he so vividly portrayed in the Francion—an exuberance which is now represented as an undesirable characteristic. Opposed to such extravagance stands Polyandre's "mesure," a value which becomes preeminent in his differentiation from Néophile.

"Mesure" does not exclude guile, which is one of the chief "attributes" of the wily Polyandre. As I pointed out earlier,

Polyandre does not hesitate to lie to Néophile: he invents part of the portrait story—stating that Néophile was Céphize's first lover—to flatter the young man's vanity (P, I, 285). As has also been discussed, Néophile is duped by Théophraste, the charlatan, and thus displays a continuing gullibility which marks him as an inferior to the perspicacious hero who is always on his guard. In general, Polyandre's allies and masters are always represented as inferiors—a situation which he accepts serenely. On the other hand, the emphasis on differentiation is more strident in the *Francion*, perhaps because indignation is more appropriate to its hero's youthful perspective.

Whatever the hero's attitude towards differentiation, the process itself tends to emphasize the importance of mixed elements in his make-up. Francion is a mischievous trickster and débauché; he is cunning and not without malice, especially when proclaiming his superiority over Clérante. Ployandre is calculating and aloof; he wears an amiable mask in society while he keeps his true objectives well hidden. In offering these morally tarnished models as his protagonists, Sorel rejected the tired perfection of earlier pulp heroes and ridiculed their behavior in the follies of Lysis. Heroes and anti-hero alike, they all act as anti-figures, as harbingers of a new form of behavior that at once overreacts to certain conventions and simultaneously points to a more reasonable, less idealized, and more "realistic" approach to the world.

If we were to sum up their distinctive traits, we would find Sorel's two heroes alike in their guile and perspicacity, qualities essential to the success of their maneuvers in society. Both, even the "noble" Francion, are largely exponents of the bourgeois ethos in which intellectual understanding and wit are more highly prized than deeds of arms and absurd passions. At the same time, if one starts out from this common core, one can point to a series of discrete elements that mark each as a profoundly different character in the service of the same ideals. Francion's outlook is colored by youth and its concomitant boldness. His curiosity is impish, and yet he is also involved in a great intellectual quest despite the comic genre: the pursuit of a new philosophy which he must conceal from all except a very select few. While he lacks Polyandre's "mesure," he shows infinitely more energy than the latter, and his occasional failures make him more interesting. Francion has a keenly developed sense of grievance; indeed, as an impoverished nobleman, he is forced to assert his innate value, to prove it to a society without discernment. His is a creative, impetuous will that forges a personality through the various vicissitudes of experience; he is a character capable of growth as well as the exponent of a particular cult of lucidity.

While Polyandre is not without ambition, his goals are more limited than Francion's: he shows no passion for any secret philosophy to assess the world; he has already reduced his knowledge to a kind of practical summary of what is necessary for self-advancement. Consequently, his social ambition is far more restrained: he slyly gains favor among the *noblesse de robe*, while the king and the *noblesse d'épée* seem totally inaccessible. In this more restricted atmosphere, tempered by age or maturity, Polyandre lacks the outrageous ebullience of Francion, but shows even more craft than his younger counterpart. Polyandre is more an exemplar of lucidity, and the restraint he shows in his dealings figures as one of the key factors differentiating him from Francion. His intellectuality is of a very different nature: he never speaks of a secret philosophy and certainly never proposes anything so daring as free love. Indeed, he never boasts of his pecadillos. His entire outlook seems social and opportunistic. Wit and amiability characterize his courting, which has none of the graphic detail of Francion's overtly carnal adventures.

Lysis' traits are evidently quite different from Francion's and Polyandre's. He has their persistence, but it is expressed in a self-defeating wrong-headedness. He is emotional but timid, if not cowardly, conniving but ineffective, verbose but not authoritative. He is a buffoon, but he does not possess the monstrous megalomania of a Hortensius. His youth and silliness render him less exasperating than the monomaniacs, who, in their turn, demonstrate some limited individual traits as well as being stereotypically unidimensional illustrations of general human failings.

## B. Monomaniacs and Madman

Monomaniacs are by far the most numerous of all Sorel's creations, and without these characters the whole notion of the comic novel would be impossible. They illustrate the various faults which afflict humanity: baseness, avarice, superstition, lechery, pedantry, etc. Most of their ills are self-inflicted, the tribute they must pay to their own unwarranted and overweening ambition. If anything, they multiply in intensity and then in numbers in Sorel's later works, for a monomaniac-madman dominates the *Berger* and the monomaniacs of the *Polyandre* outnumber Hortensius and Valentin in the *Francion.*[9] Their mode of presentation may be described as unremittingly grotesque. They are rhetorical caricatures, overdrawn creatures who often recall popular farce. Nonetheless, they are considerably differentiated from one novel to the next. Later on, in the *Polyandre*, the hero will actually proffer an analysis of the motives of their behavior—one that bespeaks a surprising tolerance and understanding. Still, even in that case one cannot speak of greater representational realism—for that was never within Sorel's understanding of realism—but simply of a moderation of the hatred and abuse directed against them in his comic novels.[10]

It is also necessary to distinguish between "monomaniacs" and "madmen" because, despite many overlapping faults, there is a critical difference between these two sets of characters, a difference which favors the mad. While Sorel quite naturally never employs the modern term *monomanie,*[11] this expression, signifying an exclusive obsession, perfectly describes a whole class of his characters. On the other hand, Sorel uses the noun/adjective *fou* exclusively as a qualifier for Collinet. Sorel also uses the word in association with Hortensius, but, as we shall see, never quite as a form of identification, but merely to suggest a state which the irascible pedant is approaching, but never actually reaches. Collinet, however, is labeled mad from his very first appearance. The critical difference between Collinet and monomaniacs like Hortensius is that the latter's tirades are consciously planned to impress others and to forward their own designs, whereas Collinet's outbursts seem to represent the purest "unreason." The monomaniacs are naïvely optimistic rather than insane and are denied the paradoxical efficacity of Collinet, who has truly lost his reason.

The problem of madness versus monomania is further complicated in the *Berger*, where Lysis is often treated as an amusing maniac and referred to as *fou*. In fact, Lysis is the most mixed of all Sorel's characters. The text is organized, from one standpoint, as a plodding movement towards his cure. But Lysis' perversity in his delusions is also underlined, and he shares in the responsibility for his condition—unlike Collinet. Nor does Lysis achieve the latter's success in social action. In a sense, Lysis is the ideal example of the merging of these two concepts before Sorel abandons madness for an exclusive concentration on monomania. Thus, as we shall see, the division between madness and monomania is most important in the *Francion*. This distinction seems to fade in the *Berger* and is without value in the *Polyandre*, where "monomania" is the only appropriate term.

The march of classicism may have had much to do with the elimination of this distinction. Sorel becomes ever more conscious of using "types" as he evolves as a comic novelist, and the types he envisions are those appropriate to an upper bourgeois setting, where court characters like the fool really have no place. Further, the rather sympathetic portrayal of some of the monomaniacs in the *Polyandre* adds a certain depth and nuance to characters of this class and perhaps obviates the need for a madman as a subtle explanation of victimization in society. The exigencies of the mature Sorel's narrative style seem to obscure and ultimately dissipate the distinction between madness and monomania, for the goals of his comic novel seemed to move towards a more tidied-up style in which a highly variable and unpredictable character like the *fou* has no place. It is in some ways a pity, for the alluring and chaotic nuances of the *Francion* vanish; the purification of the comic genre becomes its ossification.

Because of the complexity and number of monomaniacs, I shall try to proceed largely novel by novel, identifying and ana-

lyzing the characters in question. Beginning with the *Francion*,
I shall consider its two principal monomaniacs, Hortensius, the
vainglorious pedant, and Valentin, Laurette's impotent husband,
and its enigmatic madman, Collinet.[12]

Valentin's act of superstitious desperation opens the novel.
Foolishly following the advice of the "pilgrim" Francion, he
prepares a magical bath which will restore his lost potency. Without his glasses, he leaves his castle at sunset and heads for a dark
ditch, where he will be bound and inadvertently blindfolded
with his own hood. Along with these symbols of intellectual
cecity, the text concentrates a barrage of descriptive obscenity
against Valentin: the graphic details about his ravaged "zest"
and his wretched testicles underscore the futility of his quest
for potency and situate him in the tradition of classical anti-
quity's lewdest character type, the *senex*. In short, physical and
intellectual decrepitude correspond, for intellectual debility is
linked to sexual impotence. This is hardly surprising, as the libertine elite is constantly identified with youth and intelligence,
whereas the monomaniacs tend to be old and inappropriately
lecherous. All the prejudices against age are marshaled against
Sorel's monomaniac.

After uttering a particularly childish incantation, Valentin
finds himself bound to a tree. Afflicted by the monomaniac's
characteristics of superstition and fear, he believes that he is
surrounded by devils. In a comic about-face, he switches from
incantation to prayers. This tactic is reinforced by an illustration of his infantile thought processes, for he remembers the
curé's warning that one should not practice magic "si l'on ne
veut pas aller bouillir eternellement dedans la marmite d'Enfer"
(F, 70). Even the coming of dawn brings him no relief, for,
blindfolded by his hood, he imagines that the curé who addresses
him is the wily "Prince of Darkness."

Once his hood is removed, he takes stock of his situation and
realizes that he is surrounded by the local peasantry and that his
cowardice and impotence are now a matter of common knowledge. Indeed, the latter failing becomes preserved in the expression "aux bains de Valentin" (F, 86), and the whole adventure
is published. This kind of public attack is repeated, although

eventually in attenuated form, throughout all the comic novels, for the notion of an illusion game implies that being exposed as a dupe, a loser, is the most humiliating thing that can happen to any player. Such exposure is the monomaniac's constant fate.

Already Valentin displays a characteristic which will be lavishly developed in Hortensius and later in Lysis: the capacity to generate supplementary illusion from an initial deceit. By imagining that the curé is the devil, Valentin actually becomes his own duper in an infinitely expandable process of self-deception. In this self-generating process, hyperbole is the key rhetorical device, the principal source of satire.

Valentin makes only a brief reappearance, after the orgy, when he comes to Raymond's château to demand the return of his errant wife Laurette. Easily deceived, he goes home unsuccessful and his behavior thus reaffirms the theme of gullibility. His role remains that of the credulous cuckold, and his lechery affords him only frustration. The pattern of monomaniac behavior is established as constant and fruitless attempts to surpass one's condition—in Valentin's case impotence—and these futile attempts are marked by repeated humiliations.

Valentin's misadventures make up an entertaining but modest prelude to the catastrophic career of Hortensius. In fact, the latter is a kind of exemplar for all monomaniacs in the *Francion*, for he embodies the flaws of the others. Like the novel's poets, he sustains unjustified beliefs in his literary talents; like the miser, he shows the meanest kind of stinginess; like Valentin, he is also a borrowing from a traditional type—in this case, the pedant.

The implications of pedantry are manifold. The traditional pedant was always a penny-pincher. Consequently, Hortensius starves his pupils and "consoles" them with lofty but inappropriate classical citations on stoic endurance. More importantly, he is also an ignoramus, baseborn and hence, as a pedant, already above his condition. Hortensius has no real understanding of eloquence. His speeches are normally *galimatias*, a format used by monomaniacs throughout Sorel's comic works. Even his name betrays his pedantry, because, as with Valentin, the nomenclature is ironic, signifying the opposite of what it should indicate.[13]

Hortensius is a kind of anti-Francion *par excellence*, for all his misadventures form a complete contrast to the successes of the hero. In fact, he may be described as a negative of the hero, for the two are paired in a typically baroque juxtaposition of opposites.[14] This opposition is not based simply on attitudes and generalized behavior patterns. It goes even further in elaborate contrasts between certain specific episodes to form sets representing the ideal and the nadir of social comportment.

One of the most dramatic extended contrasts between the two is Hortensius' courtship of Frémonde, which can be viewed in juxtaposition with the courtship of Nays and Francion's courting in general. Hortensius' maneuvers are a distortion of Francion's normal courting procedures. Like the hero's love for Nays, Hortensius' passion originated from an artificial source: not a portrait this time, but the romantic novels the pedant has confiscated from the young Francion. Little need be said about the negative role Sorel ascribed to novels; any passion arising from such reading is condemned from the outset. Following the rituals of courtship described in ch. 1,[15] Hortensius takes the first step with a display of his literary talents to his intended. His missive, however, is not an elegant *poulet*, but a *galimatias*— and a plagiarized one at that:

> . . . tous les jours il fueilletoit les livres d'amour qu'il m'avoit pris, et tiroit les discours qui estoient les meilleurs a son jugement pour orner doresnavant sa bouche. Entre ses volumes, il y en avoit un plein de Metamorphores, d'Antitheses barbares, de figures si extraordinaires qu'on ne leur peut donner de nom, et d'un galimatias continuel où le plus subtil esprit du monde fust demeuré a quia . . . . (F, 189)

With his language "adorned" with the worst abuses of contemporary literature, Hortensius conquers, but for the wrong reasons. Frémonde, the mistress of his affections, retains him as an object of amusement—a foreshadowing of his treatment by Francion and Nays. This procedure is again commonplace. The monomaniac assumes the role of dupe when he would like to play the manipulator. A would-be subject, he becomes the object by an automatic turning of the tables. The situation might be termed a loss of control by a character who maintains a belief in his own autonomy.

Hortensius' failure at the elegant use of language is carried over into the other aspects of courtship. Traditionally, the suitor should demonstrate his generosity, and so Hortensius offers a feast for Frémonde. This collation naturally only demonstrates his stinginess, gluttony, and intemperance. Having easily become intoxicated, he performs an "academic" ballet in which he dances the role of the principal of his *collège* with whip in hand. The detail actually provides telling commentary on his true role with his students. When the drunken Hortensius is caught by the real principal, his pathetic feast ends on a note of complete embarrassment which reveals him not as the master of a well-planned celebration, but as an incompetent bumbler unable to control the course of events. The whole episode may be read as a crude version of Francion's legitimate panache and verbal dexterity in courting Nays. Again, following a baroque format, the novel offers both extremes of human behavior.

A consistent element in the courting ritual is the necessity to deceive a guardian. Francion, through varied ruses, always has his way. In the Frémonde episode, this obstacle is seen in the need for Hortensius to establish his social standing with Frémonde and her lawyer, i.e., to present a "preuve de noblesse" to win consent to the marriage. Aware of the pedant's pretensions, Frémonde and the lawyer go along with the game. Their questioning of Hortensius and their cross-examination of his inept peasant corroborator lead to the shocking revelation that Hortensius was originally a swineherd. What happens to Hortensius here is part of an automatic mechanism: whenever a monomaniac seeks social advancement, his ruses turn viciously against him and bring about his total humiliation. Taunted, he storms off with his useless finery—most notably a sword to indicate his nobility. Again, his pathetic display contrasts with the elegance that accompanies Francion's courtship. Not even the externals of rank are sufficient to conceal his innate inferiority.

The Frémonde episode focuses on Hortensius' gravest transgression: the violation of class boundaries. In fact, this transgression is at the heart of all of his problems because it indicates his most serious flaw: the desire to be what he is not, the refusal to accept reality whether it be a matter of his intellectual abilities or, more importantly, his social standing.[16] Here Sorel's prejudices come into play, for, although the *Francion* may be thought of as bourgeois literature, it would be erroneous to represent Sorel as the advocate of social ascension for his class or the lower orders. Like most of his contemporaries, he accepted the various gradations of society. His own attempt at social advancement came not from a belief in the right of the competent bourgeois to social elevation, but rather from a spurious attempt to establish his own nobility.[17] While the *Francion* does reflect subconsciously very definite bourgeois attitudes, it upholds an extremely conservative social order. An individual is born into a certain class and he may ascend no farther. The arrogance of attempting social ascension is Hortensius' unpardonable crime and the source of nearly all his woes. From the onset, he is represented as a climber. Driven by venality, Hortensius and his like ". . . sont des gents qui viennent presque de la charruë a la chaire" (F, 184). The greed that pushed him into "education" attests to his literal as well as figurative lack of "generosity," the attribute of a man of quality.[18] Conservatively, the novel rejects Hortensius' every attempt to free himself from his class. His very ambition will push him close to insanity, make him an easy mark for tricksters, and ultimately render him a victim of his own self-deception.

Hortensius' unsuccessful struggle upwards meets with unvarying humiliation. Twice, he tries to pass for a noble: first, in the Frémonde episode, by wearing a sword and, on another occasion, when, out of sheer arrogance, he dons riding boots "pour paroistre Gentilhomme" (F, 413). Each situation ends in an embarrassing failure. Later on, his "friends" humor him in the "Polish ambassador" episode by fooling Hortensius into thinking he has been chosen king of Poland. Only too willing to believe in his royal destiny, the fulfillment of his wildest dreams, he tries to dupe himself and begins to doubt the previously unquestioned baseness of his origins: "et puis l'on trouvera a la fin paravanture que je suis encore plus que je n'ay estimé. Voyez dans tous les Romans les belles recognoissances qu'il y a" (F, 448).

This allusion to novels as if they contained historical precedents already indicates partial derangement, for it signifies an acquiescence to fiction over reality. In fact, Hortensius' near dementia was already prefigured in the student play episode and the Saluste misadventure. In the first instance, Francion greeted the pedant's arrival on stage with the telling verse: "Que viens tu faire icy, animal sans raison?" (F, 186). In the second instance, the poet Saluste, whom Hortensius had unwittingly thrown out of his quarters, concluded that Hortensius was "un fou aussi furieux qu'il y en eust aux petites maisons" (F, 413). While Hortensius will never go totally mad, he will come dangerously close. Audebert, for instance, keeps vigil with Hortensius with the express purpose of driving him insane: "il esperoit qu'a force de veiller et de parler de choses extravagantes, Hortensius deviendroit entierement fou" (F, 442). Without ever passing a final verdict of complete folly, the King of Poland episode illustrates that unwarranted ambition is the nemesis of reason. The social climber is ready to persuade himself that the impossible is true. But class structure in the novel remains immutable. And so, for his brashness, Hortensius is transformed into an unwitting buffoon, a clown king condemned to await futilely the return of the vanished ambassadors.

## Collinet, the Madman

Up to this point, we have discussed two monomaniacs in the *Francion*, Valentin and Hortensius, and we have shown that the efforts of these characters to surpass their conditions—sexual impotence and base birth—end inevitably in failure. In every case, Valentin and Hortensius become objects of amusement for others. Collinet would seem to have some affinity with these two because, from his first appearance in the novel, he plays the role of buffoon for Clérante's court. Yet there are few grounds for likening him to any of the novel's principal monomaniacs, for his madness is curiously lucid: it often prefigures events, recognizes a critical issue, or chastises a truly offensive character.

Collinet is initially presented as entirely mad. Little information is supplied on the development of his madness. However, the few comments that are made on the subject place him in an entirely different category from Hortensius. Apparently a former lawyer, Collinet is not cast as a charlatan, although this is the usual fate for men of the law in the novel.[19] Rather, he is portrayed as a respectable gentleman who lost his mind after being ruined in a legal case; i.e., he is a victim of the legal system, rather than a perpetrator of that system. Several elements are important here. Collinet's madness is in no way linked to an attempt to move beyond his social station. He seems to have been a well-educated bourgeois. He is never identified as a commoner suffering from delusions of grandeur. Secondly, Collinet is associated by implication with the hero's father, who was himself thoroughly victimized by legal chicanery (F, 156-64): Collinet is thus "related" to the hero by analogical experience. Finally, the illusion game which governs the novel's intrigues imposes an inevitable symbiosis of dupes and tricksters. Even Francion himself is not always on the winning side. Collinet may well represent the hero as victim.

The notion of the hero-victim, although it may seem a bit strained when applied to the *Francion*, is reinforced by Lysis' situation in the *Berger*, for Lysis has lost his mind not from any vain attempt at social ascension, but merely from uncritically reading too many novels. Thus, whether used for legal chicanery or romantic nonsense, language for Sorel is fraught with danger for mental balance. Any man may fall victim to its wiles, and, since it holds the key to reality, when abused it may drive men mad. Collinet's insanity may well be Sorel's observation on the negative power of the word.

But beyond warning his reader about the dangers of the word, Sorel clearly had more positive uses for Collinet. To wit, this avid reader and author of an evaluation of contemporary French literature probably had the tradition of the wise fool in mind when he created Collinet. As Foucault indicates, the character of the fool had already assumed a paradoxically knowledgeable role in the theater of the late Middle Ages.[20]

In many ways Collinet embodies the traditional fool, most especially in speaking the truth in obscure or crazed language. His ranting discourses are always distortions of a particular kind of language—courtly parlance. His tirades constitute a microcosm of the novel's procedure of juxtaposing the grandiose and the vulgar. Witness, for instance, Collinet's discourses to Luce and later to Raymond's Héleine. Both begin with extraordinary courtly respect, but rapidly transform themselves into obscene ranting which underscores the ultimate relationships between the two women and their admirers. Collinet is the buffoon who has the last laugh.

Further in keeping with the tradition of the fool, Collinet offers excellent advice and enjoys the jester's privilege of impunity. He instructs Clérante on the treatment of flatterers (F, 257) and discourages his bellicose inclinations (F, 258-59). Profiting from the immunity of folly, Collinet avenges Francion's grievances by beating the hated Melibée (F, 1298-99, "Variantes") and a troublesome paymaster (F, 261-62). Furthermore, Collinet has a keen wit: he coins ferociously obscene puns with deftness. In the very success of his aggressiveness, Collinet distinguishes himself from the wretched Valentin and Hortensius, whose designs meet with constant failure.

Even Collinet's apparently spontaneous attacks are signaled as acts of lucidity: ". . . il sert merveilleusement a combattre l'orgueil de tant de viles ames qui sont en France, et lesquelles il sçait bien cognoistre par une faculté que la nature a imprimée en luy" (F, 262). An instinctive knowledge seems to have supplanted the reasoning skills which characters normally require to maneuver in the illusion game. Collinet is strangely compensated for his insanity: he may still make the right choice, even though the detective faculties required for playing the illusion game are theoretically impaired. Thus, despite his insanity, Collinet actually resembles a slightly distorted version of the hero Francion.

Clearly, total madness cannot be considered a damning flaw. What is negative, however, is the megalomania which results from overweening social ambition. When a character seeks to move beyond his station, then an inexorable process is set in motion which brings him to the brink of insanity—not the holy madness of times past, but a frenzied simulacrum of folly which leads the climber to continuous humiliation. Sorel implies that this near madness destroys because it is generated by a perverse quest for illusion, i.e., by the free play of vanity ready to dupe itself to achieve some truly impossible objective.

Sorel creates an engaging paradox by allowing a prisoner of illusion to come closest to the most lucid character of the novel. This paradox suggests certain aspects of the relationship between reality and illusion within the *Francion*. They are, of course, interdependent concepts, rich in baroque ambivalence. All characters seek to be deceivers, although most are deceived. Few seem totally lucid: even the hero occasionally plays the *trompeur trompé*. Collinet may be the instrument which Sorel uses to draw these diverse currents together, the symbol of an instinctive perception which transcends the characteristic juxtaposition of illusion and reality. Indeed, without a middle or shaded ground, the baroque consciousness moves immediately to polarization: to paradox in lieu of synthesis. Collinet is at distinct levels a rhetorical figure and a philosophical resolution of contradictions.

Lysis-Louis[21] inherits much from Collinet as well as from the monomaniacs of the *Francion*, for he incorporates the sympathetic aspects of the former while he is abused in a manner more similar to the latter, most especially Hortensius. In creating this extraordinary madman,[22] Sorel had multiple goals. He was not so much attacking people with pretensions above their stations or would-be authors whose ignorance was unparalleled.[23] Rather, in attacking all novels, he needed a character who, unlike Hortensius, could conserve a certain limited measure of sympathy so that the indictment of literature would not become excessively personal and ineffectively specific. On the other hand, Sorel must have felt a certain fascination for the character Hortensius, for he took the particular pattern of abuse applied to him and made it the general pattern for the *Berger*. That novel seems to have been prepared almost simultaneously with the second edition of the *Francion*—an edition which featured the return of Hortensius. It is possible that Sorel may have been responding to reader demand. Whatever the case, Hortensius does serve as the prototype for a particular kind of satirical structure. But the inspiration for the character Lysis can hardly be said to have originated exclusively in the *Francion*. The allusions to *Don Quixote* both in the *Berger* and in the *Polyandre* make it clear not only that Sorel found inspiration in the pages of Cervantes, but also that he saw the Spaniard as a rival.[24] The creation of a mad shepherd whose adventures surpassed those of the deranged knight was one of Sorel's objectives.

Sorel's principal technique in the presentation of Lysis is an emphasis on the distortion of vision. The bizarre shepherd first appears reciting an apostrophe to his flock and praising the virtues of his beloved Charite. Hardly has Lysis finished his tirade when the narrator adds that his sheep are "brebis galeuses, qui n'estoient que le rebut des bouchers de Poissy" (BE, 19). From the onset, Lysis' vision is represented as a grotesque misrepresentation of reality. Sorel is forever balancing an unsavory reality with the idealized hyperbole of Lysis' demented imagination. The latter's perversity is immediately comprehended by Anselme and his friends, and their reaction is to play along with Lysis' manias exactly as Francion's circle exploited Hortensius's royalist fantasies.

But Lysis also has much in common with Collinet. There is no class problem: he is a bourgeois, not a peasant. His madness does not spring from his overweening social pretensions; rather, he too is the victim of others, not lawyers, but the authors of his time. Even Francion admits that, as a *collégien*, he fell prey to the allure of novels which he read in preference to his texts.[25] It is thus hardly astonishing that a person of limited discernment should succumb to the snares of novelists. The *Berger* is a very extended development of this entrapment by literature. Unlike the *Francion*, its hero undergoes no struggle for perception. The *Berger* is uniquely the novel of the victim—quasi sympathetic—whose personal resources are insufficient to deliver him from his folly. Because the boundaries between illusion and reality are perhaps too clear, because Lysis is not engaged in any progressive struggle towards perspicacity, the novel is weak.[26] There is none of the spice of the *trompeur trompé*, only an eventual *deus ex machina* in the person of Clarimond, who will deliver Lysis from his illusions.

Lysis' madness is thus qualitatively different from Collinet's. The former's perceptions are always inaccurate; the instinct of Collinet is totally absent. Lysis is neither rhetorically nor philosophically a fusion of *être* and *paraître*. Nor does his madness seem to have any connection with older, more sacred notions of folly. On the contrary, he is a purely satirical device created to demonstrate every foible, every absurdity of contemporary literature.

A unique aspect of Lysis' monomania is his literal-mindedness. The young bourgeois is not unread; in fact, he is a storehouse of mythological knowledge. He explains all phenomena entirely upon the basis of the classical heritage. As a result, he can be lured into endless arguments by Anselme and the others —arguments whose sole result is the explosion of Lysis' tenets by their own extended absurdity. In a sense, an early modern scientific attitude is evident in this form of satire, for Sorel understood that simplicity provided the most valid explanation.[27] He uses Lysis' obsessive vision as a vehicle for ridiculing outmoded explanations of phenomena and hackneyed attitudes towards love. The classical heritage, thus assailed, degenerates into superstition, cliché, an absurd system of nonsense unduly revered and uncritically accepted.

Sorel's approach to the monomaniacs in the *Polyandre* is considerably different. First of all, he returns to a narrative with a true hero and thus eliminates the exclusive focus on the monomaniac as the center of all action. Second, Sorel introduces a host of monomaniacs in the *Polyandre*. The principal ones include Musigène, the *poète crotté*; Orilan, the *amant universel*; Gastrimargue, the parasitic pedant; and Héliodore-Théophraste, the charlatan. Obviously, Sorel felt the need to multiply his characters to give a greater variety of obsessions. But even a superficial reading reveals that there are vast differences between the older Sorel's monomaniacs and those he created in the *Francion*. For one thing, though full of faults, they are not entirely repugnant creatures: Musigène and Orilan enjoy what appears to be a genuine friendship with the hero, while Gastrimargue remains a more consistent victim and enemy. In fact, Polyandre explains the general plight of all monomaniacs to Néophile as he instructs the latter in the ways of the world and goes so far as to justify their behavior:

Au contraire ceux qui sont pauvres des biens de fortune, & n'ont pas aussi les dons de nature les plus exquis, sont forcez la pluspart du temps de mener une vie toute extraordinaire; & il y en a tel qui faisant le foû y trouve mieux son compte que s'il faisoit le sage. Combien pensez-vous qu'il y a de gens dans Paris, qui ne seroient pas si bien venus chez les Grands s'ils ne vivoient de quelque façon hétéroclite? (P, I, 156)

Thus, in Polyandre's analysis, Orilan and Musigène are using a kind of self-interested stratagem which deliberately overdoes courtship and poetry in the hope that their very curious behavior will generate some kind of self-advancement. Clearly, the notion of the monomaniac as the dogged self-deceiver has been modified. The monomaniacs have now become very self-conscious players; they lucidly take on the role of fool to pluck whatever advantage they can obtain from it. There is a new awareness of the human need for the grotesque conferred upon these characters, and they become more actors than objects. They do not need Collinet's instinctive prescience to make their way in the world. Perhaps Sorel in his maturity sought a new dimension for the monomaniacs, one that was better adapted to a novel of mores because of the higher level of consciousness in all its characters.

This alteration is apparent in their fate. Musigène is relatively well treated. His stories are heard with enthusiasm. In fact, it is he who recounts the first tale of Gastrimargue, and hence he acquires a power normally denied to the monomaniac: the satirical abuse of others. Musigène also receives a financial gift from Aesculan which indicates that his verbal abilities are not totally without merit. Orilan, while he is vain, aggressive, impetuous, and frequently the butt of many jokes, still manages to fare relatively well. For instance, during a ball, Polyandre plays a practical joke on him: he has Orilan's red wig lifted to the ceiling. But unlike the monomaniacs of the *Francion*, Orilan turns the tables: through his wit and graciousness he wins a certain degree of admiration.[28] Contrary to the normal laws of automatic humiliation, he shows that he has the mental resources to triumph in a potentially degrading situation. Again, this turnabout is related to the upgrading of the monomaniac, an effort to add dimension to this class of characters.

This change is, however, not universal. Héliodore-Théophraste, the charlatan, is seen in a predominantly negative light and his schemes usually end in failure. It is interesting to note, however, that only flawed characters like Clorinie, the coquette, and Néophile, the apprentice at love, are fooled by his ruses. Otherwise, he encounters failure, as in the alchemy and Rosicrucian episodes. Gastrimargue is perhaps the most loathsome and enigmatic of all the monomaniacs. He is gluttonous, lecherous, avaricious, and vain. He is singled out for exceptional abuse: three separate stories all portray him in exceedingly humiliating circumstances.[29] Yet the last news of Gastrimargue is bewilderingly excellent: a wealthy gentleman has taken pity on him and compensated Gastrimargue for the loss of his miserable carriage and nag with a far finer vehicle and team as well as with a vast income. Musigène is obviously exceedingly depressed by his enemy's unwarranted windfall. Since the novel was never completed, one can only speculate on Sorel's ultimate intentions. The author clearly had no sympathy for Gastrimargue. Was his sudden good fortune just another peripeteia to stimulate curiosity, a situation which was to be reversed in the next volume?[30] Or was it a lesson to the reader, an implication that society is full of successful cheats? In the *Francion*, the monomaniacs never came out on top. Was Sorel trying to be more realistic by showing the success of the most unworthy character of the novel? This may well be the case. Héliodore knows qualified success (enough at least to keep him going) and Gastrimargue actually becomes wealthy. Sorel may be acknowledging that the monomaniacs are also capable of being successful players in the illusion game, and their very success would be an acrimonious criticism of human stupidity as well as a more subtle portrayal of the workings of society than he had drawn in the *Francion*.

Clearly, the chief function of Sorel's monomaniacs is to aid in the unfolding of the narrative process by figuring as polar opposites to the heroes or at least to serve as illustrations of human failings. Though they are modified as Sorel's writing develops, they do not undergo a radical change of function, just a gradual modification which includes a less negative portrayal in certain cases. Nevertheless, they do possess distinctive character traits, which, elaborated within their overall narrative functions, set off the various monomaniacs from each other.

In the *Francion*, Valentin's particular inferiority lies in the domain of sexual impotence, and his readiness to be duped is expressed concretely in his resort to magical remedies to overcome his sexual insufficiencies. He is one of the most physically presented of all the monomaniacs, for he is marked by ravaged genitalia, defects of vision, and presumably old age. In short, he is particularly characterized by a loathsome corporality. He thus conforms to the narrative pattern which assigns him a contrapuntal role to libertine youth and vigor, a pattern which opposes superstitious credulity to inquiring intelligence.

Hortensius has an extensively depicted array of flaws, but his chief character traits—beyond the omnipresent inclination to self-deception—are his appalling greed, raging temper, and unbridled egomania. His unshakable faith in his authorial talents marks him as the most conceited of the monomaniacs in the *Francion*. Further, his extraordinary fits of temper mesh perfectly with his overblown conception of self. Verbosity—somewhat limited in Valentin—is the natural avenue for the expression of his "learning," for, as the anti-author, he rains torrents of misused words and expressions to demonstrate both his own incompetence in language and the weaknesses of contemporary literature.

In short, both Valentin and Hortensius are classical types—the *senex* and the pedant—and their characterization, while it is developed according to a rather time-honored format, is used in the service of a new literary ideology. Collinet, although he belongs to a traditional typology inasmuch as he plays the role of the *fou*, remains set apart from these two. He is zany and explosive and acts as Francion's comic ally. He is a boisterous but good-willed creature with a maniac vitality, somehow used in the service of good. Lysis, whom I have already characterized, inherits only Collinet's deficiencies, for which he receives much less sympathy.

In the *Polyandre*, as indicated, Gastrimargue resurrects many of the loathsome characteristics of Hortensius. Once more, an "author" of explosive vanity, total avarice, unparalleled gluttony, and unstinted verbosity figures as a whipping boy for Sorel's satire of contemporary literature. As the most reprehensible of the novel's monomaniacs, Gastrimargue undergoes the most brutal humiliations, to which he responds with characteristic baseness. Typology, however, does differentiate Gastrimargue from Hortensius because, if he represents most dominantly any one classical type, it is surely the parasite, as witnessed by the lavish, Rabelaisian pages devoted to his appetite. He is not only a dismal pedant, but he also very closely resembles a kind of eating machine of extraordinary ingestive capacities. He is thus at once all-consuming and unproductive.

Héliodore-Théophraste is the other of the monomaniacs in the *Polyandre* with no redeeming traits. He has the personality of an experienced, if not thoroughly competent, operator, as much his own victim as a victimizer. Cunning and cajoling, he is clearly a mythomaniac, capable of spinning the most far-fetched tales at the scent of ill-gotten gain. Again, he belongs to a specific type: the charlatan.

Musigène is a "newer" monomaniac: he is surprisingly amiable, an amusing and gifted storyteller. He frequently accompanies the hero and on several occasions acts as a kind of joking sidekick. He is very changeable in moods, going from elation at the prospect of buying new clothes to depression over his enemy Gastrimargue's financial success. He also has a streak of dandyism about him—a logical feature, given the tattered clothing in which he appears at the opening of the novel. He clearly represents a type: the *poète crotté* and also figures as part of the satire of language. Nevertheless, he remains a sympathetic creature, more to be pitied than reviled.

Orilan, like Musigène, elicits as much sympathy as disapprobation. He is always fantastic and outrageous in his hyperbolic proposals to nearly every woman he encounters. His antics are, however, part of a conscious buffoonery rather than unconscious spectacle. He shows an abundant energy in his innumerable amorous quests, which mark him as fiery and feisty. But he is extraordinarily literate as well—a fact amply illustrated in his debate with Musigène, during which he maintains his superiority as a lover to Lysis and to Hylas, the inconstant shepherd of the *Astrée*. He even has a measure of dignity, as witnessed by his behavior at the ball. Like the others, he becomes a type—

*l'amant universel*—enlisted in Sorel's satirical treatment of absurd passions.


   While a discussion of characters and their traits could be prolonged indefinitely, an examination of the heroes and monomaniacs of Sorel's novels really covers the essentials of his system and its development. The most important relationship is one of diametrical opposition: ignorance versus lucidity, impotence versus power. The format was clearly established in the *Francion* and reaffirmed in the *Berger*, where almost all emphasis was on willful self-deception. While the *Polyandre* basically uses the same system, it does slightly attenuate this radical opposition by adding certain characters with mixed traits, namely, monomaniacs with a minimal lucidity. The *Polyandre* is more a comedy of manners, but it ultimately presents the same world view as the other works—only with a trifle more indulgence for its dupes. Yet it would be a mistake to look for any psychological realism in Sorel's personae, even with their evolution in the *Polyandre*. Indeed, his characters were never meant to be realistic in the current sense of the term. They derive largely from stock types and have the familiarity of figures to which Sorel's audience was long accustomed. More than personalities, they are extended narratological messages—either comically edifying examples, as in the case of the heroes, or humorous warnings, as illustrated by the plights of the various monomaniacs. Their similarity within their respective groupings is due to their elaboration along the polarities of lucidity and blindness. In fact, characterization is, in one respect, yet another element in the coherence of Sorel's novels. Like the minor intrigues of the *Francion*, characterization offers a subtle variation in a message which remains constant. Sorel's personae are not "human" in the sense of later characters in nineteenth- and twentieth-century fiction; rather, they are the textual devices of an ardent reformer of literary and social abuse.

*Chapter III*

## DISGUISE AND ITS ANALOGUES
## IN LANGUAGE AND PORTRAITURE

The tension between *être* and *paraître* marks all of Sorel's comic novels. Deceit, treachery, and astute maneuvers are part and parcel of the illusion game, which in turn governs their intrigues in their entirety by regulating all relationships between characters, by making all social activity a contest of perception. In such an atmosphere, the abundance of disguise should come as no surprise. Logically, this profusion of costume has its analogues in language and portraiture, for language can hide the truth in lies, and portraiture can falsify reality as easily as it represents it. Perhaps the key device in setting off lucidity against dupery, disguise enjoys a unique place in Sorel's comic novels, for its sweep is exceptionally vast, extending not simply to heroes alone, but to a host of other characters as well.

In approaching the subject, we shall first examine disguise by assessing the sociological function of clothing as perceived by Sorel and then move on to the practical application of disguise in the individual novels. Then we shall consider language to show how it follows patterns discernible in masquerade. Finally, we shall demonstrate how portraiture reflects similar patterns and, by doing so, illustrate the coherence of divergent aspects of the comic novels.

## The Role of Clothing

In order to place disguise in its proper perspective, it is worthwhile to examine Sorel's understanding of the function of clothing as elaborated in the youthful Francion's apprenticeship in the ways of the world.[1] Although the subject is not specifically masquerade, the account of Francion's financial distress in Paris supplies an interpretation of the role of clothing which nearly merges *être* and *paraître*. In a series of three misadventures, the impoverished Francion, forced to dress in tatters, learns that his quality has become invisible as he meets with rebuff from representatives of each of the three estates.

In the first of these encounters, Francion tries to reproach a merchant's son and former classmate for carrying a sword. Although Francion is a genuine member of the *noblesse d'épée*, he is treated as rabble by this imposter and forced to make a humiliating retreat (F, 215-16). On the second occasion, Francion is tormented by a page, the implied catamite of a homosexual baron. The hero's efforts to defend himself are thwarted by the baron's intervention. Once again, he is dismissed as riffraff because of his tattered clothing (F, 220). Finally, a priest tries to exclude him from vespers because of his shabby attire. Only here does Francion's reprimand have any effect, perhaps because heavenly matters, being extrasocial, ought not to fall under the rules of appearance (F, 222). (It might even be argued that, given the priest's attitude, they actually do.) In any event, the lesson Francion learns from these experiences, even in what should be the charitable domain of religion, is that clothes make the man. However corrupt such an outlook may be, all must acquiesce to society's clumsy and superficial manner of judging.[2]

And so, when Francion is sent money by his mother, he immediately transforms himself by donning the costume of his rank and is thereafter treated accordingly. With the appropriate trappings, he is free to take his place in society. But the lesson is learned: not even the hero can place himself above the laws of appearance, for quality must be visible or go unacknowledged. Deprivation of appropriate garb is a kind of death, just as donning a new costume becomes a birth into a new form of life.

Even the ragged Musigène, the poet of the *Polyandre*, is well aware of such cultural imperatives. Aesculan's largesse immediately sets him to thinking about the clothes he will purchase. Musigène explains to Polyandre "qu'il aymoit l'honneur du monde, qui consistoit dans l'aparance des choses exterieures" (P, I, 373). At the very beginning of the novel, Musigène appears with his apparel literally falling apart. In this context, his remark is not a haphazard observation, but an expression of belief that he can overcome his wretched condition by a change of clothes. Musigène understands the relationship between appearance and social standing, even if his remarks are presented comically.

In a similar vein, Lysis knows that he cannot live the pastoral without disguising himself as a shepherd, nor does he believe that he can play the role of conquering hero without appropriate, antiquely styled garments. From the maddest to the wisest, all of Sorel's comic characters understand the critical importance of costume. The less lucid believe that clothing alone determines essence.

At times, clothing can be used to change social station, to misrepresent intentions, in short, to dupe the rest of the world. The focus of Sorel's realism is its cynicism about human perception. For him, humanity clearly lacked discernment, and, at one level, the abundance of disguise is an amusing lesson on human stupidity and gullibility. Its numerous apparitions are the natural responses of characters anxious to take every advantage of other players.

## Disguise

In order to analyze disguise, its manifestations have been divided into several categories. The first is composed of the characters in Sorel's work who may be called heroes, Francion and Polyandre. The second is made up of Lysis, who will be considered as an intermediate figure between the heroes and the monomaniacs, and those who exploit his follies (Anselme, Hircan, etc.). The last group consists exclusively of the monomaniacs.

Francion

Francion dons a number of costumes: he first appears as a pilgrim, then as an itinerant musician, after that as a wafer-maker,[3] next as a peasant, and finally as a quack. What commands attention in this profusion of costume is the frequent association of disguise with the notions of death and resurrection. Indeed, in four particular instances the hero is threatened with imminent death, and his threatened doom and eventual deliverance are dramatically associated with a change of costume: first in his escape from Count Bajamond's assassins, then at the beginning of the orgy, later during his liberation from the fortress in Book IX, and finally in the confusion of identities between Francion and the old conspirator in Book X. All of these episodes elucidate the relationship between disguise and death and resurrection, as well as the other functions of the hero's masquerade.

We first meet Francion masquerading as a pilgrim—a richly polyvalent costume which engenders a pun: he is on a pilgrimage to "nostre dame de Lorette." It also underlines Francion's role as a wanderer in search of a goal, emphasizes the constant physical displacement which characterizes the novel, and successfully enables Francion to play the part of trickster by duping the credulous Valentin. It is further a preliminary to the death and resurrection episodes created by his other masquerades because it focuses on a nearly fatal fall as a dramatic device to illustrate Francion's learning process in the use of disguise. Masquerade and death are joined here when Francion is shaken to the ground by the thief Olivier in his attempt to scale the castle wall to reach Laurette, his paramour. He lands in Valentin's tun, where, unconscious and bleeding profusely, he is disgracefully associated with the latter's impotence. But the most significant aspect of this misadventure is that the Laurette whom Francion idolizes is, in fact, a rapacious tart awaiting anxiously not his love, but the gift of an expensive emerald ring. Francion's pilgrimage to "nostre dame de Lorette" is made under false auspices. Thus, the near-fatal fall from the castle wall is a kind of punishment. And so, despite his actual success in duping Valentin, this episode must be viewed as basically negative, and the use of disguise is associated with failure, which almost ends in death.

In the raggamuffin musician episode, in which the hero mingles with and abuses the local peasantry, Francion uses disguise as a way to amuse his patron Clérante. The pretext for the adventure is to enjoy the foolishness of a peasant marriage ceremony and to enable Clérante to win the favors of a local bourgeoise without revealing his true identity. Disguise supposedly functions as a shield, a license to misbehave in a group of inferiors. There are several points worthy of note in this masquerade. First of all, it is one of the devices which permit Sorel to give the novel a social breadth: the costumes become passports into the world of the lower orders. Second, as previously indicated, the whole episode supplies a grotesque counterpart for the lofty ceremonies of the orgy: marriage is degraded as an institution fit only for the "terrestres et brutaux." Sorel depicts the peasant world as one of crudity and total inferiority. The masquerade thus enables him to snipe at the pastoral by providing a picture of rural life marred by filth and ignorance.[4] Grotesque costuming here bolsters this willfully crude portrayal of peasant inferiority and contributes to the antithesis of the libertine ideal. Disguise also underlines Francion's role as a prankster capable of manipulating appearances at will, and it gives him the opportunity to exhibit one of his many talents: in this case, playing the fiddle.

Near the end of Book VI and almost immediately before the libertine orgy, Francion narrowly escapes death from a band of assassins in the pay of the ignoble Count Bajamond. He saves himself by dressing up as a wafer-maker in order to fool his would-be murderers. This costume obviously initiates a strong association between disguise and death and resurrection, since it delivers Francion from almost certain assassination. Further, it also represents a *tour de force* because he is later arrested in his disguise as a suspicious character and nevertheless manages to extricate himself from his captors without revealing his identity, a measure which he disdains as too facile. Instead, he bribes the "Archers" and safely returns to the pastry shop to give back his disguise and obtain his original clothes. This brief episode is thus a demonstration through costume of Francion's protean fluidity and practical intelligence: disguise gets him out of trouble and then into trouble once more, a new situation which he overcomes with ease. But most importantly, the initial success of this disguise suggests that mastery of illusion may be equated with triumph over death.

The libertine orgy, which follows closely upon this episode, will renew this association of disguise with death and resurrection, this time through Count Raymond's peculiar joke. On the eve of this revel, feigning offense at Francion's allegation of an old theft, Raymond storms out of his room with the threat of a reckoning on the morrow. The next day, the wounded Francion, who is dressed *à l'antique* as a kind of sacrificial victim, assumes that he is to be put to death. Of course, he finds that what awaits him is not execution, but an invitation to be an honored guest at this elitist feast. This surprise reversal of a supposedly fatal situation effects a kind of resurrection. Francion has been "reborn" as a libertine philosopher.

There are several aspects which distinguish this masquerade from all others in the novel. First of all, costuming is not contemporary; second, this is the only masquerade during which Francion does not descend to a lower social station when using costume; third, it is the only masquerade during which no one is duped. In fact, the other revelers are similarly attired. Disguise becomes richly suggestive. Antique garb appropriately brings to mind the Petronian legacy and confers some of the lofty dignity of the philosophic and literary traditions of the ancient world upon Francion's call for a refined vocabulary of love and universal sexual freedom. This particular masquerade actually rises to the occasion of Francion's "rebirth": instead of concealing the person beneath it, disguise works a paradoxical merger of *être* and *paraître*. Francion's costume enables him to transcend the mundane, to enter the lofty empyrean of libertine speculation.

It is significant that this use of masquerade and resurrection occurs after Francion has completed his apprenticeship in lucidity, at the very close of the first edition of the novel. He is now fully aware that Laurette is a prostitute and that her conquest offers no special distinction. He has been restored from the near-fatal blindness of his infatuation and has "arisen" from ignorance, ready to face the world as a full-fledged trickster. As for Francion's relationship to others, the normal rules of the illusion game must be suspended because the libertine elite cannot be duped. Francion is among his own and costume may play only an amplifying role. Costume becomes the uniform of the elite, the symbol of collective assent to Francion's libertine apotheosis.

On the other hand, the death and resurrection theme may also introduce a certain reserve into the libertine setting. The evocation of death before indulgence in pleasure may be viewed either as a stimulant or as a note of caution on the limits of sensual delight.[5] Certainly, Sorel reiterates the notion of death within the episode, for he includes the decrepit Agathe in the festivities. Here, implicitly at least, the old hag seems to be viewed as a stimulant, a baroque *carpe diem* injunction: enjoy the present moment, the revelers are told, for she represents the physical corruption which awaits them all (F, 314). On the other hand, Francion's own melancholy reflections, suppressed at Raymond's insistence, may well suggest some misgivings about the adequacies of pleasure, misgivings which exploit his general association of death and costume:

"Mesme nous autres, qui croyons avoir bien employé le temps que nous passons a l'amour, aux festins, aux mommeries, nous nous trouverrons a la fin trompez: nous verrons que nous sommes des fous. Les maladies nous affligeront et la debilité des membres nous viendra, avant que nous soyons en l'age caduc." (F, 312)

In any event, this mixture of morbidity and delight gives an impression of ambiguity and perhaps illustrates the underlying malaise of contemporary libertines.

Though the orgy is a triumph which establishes in emphatic terms Francion's complete lucidity and his deliverance from the empire of amorous illusion, it is by no means the last illustration of the hero's new-found power. On the contrary, Francion's successes will be echoed throughout the text, most especially in the two other disguise incidents which incorporate the death and resurrection motif.

In the first, Francion foolishly tries a "magic" chair at the behest of his rivals and finds himself imprisoned for his gullibility.

He is delivered from captivity by being placed blindfolded into a boat which he mistakes for a bier (F, 366). Shortly, he finds himself "reborn" not into a world of libertine refinement, but rather into one of bucolic crudity. In effect, several registers are played on here. One inevitably thinks of Céladon, who casts himself into the Lignon to be found ragged, filthy, and half drowned by a trio of nymphs.[6] Francion is about to embark on a pastoral adventure—or rather a satire on the pastoral which will be expanded in *Le Berger extravagant*. His death and resurrection are, from this point of view, entirely sarcastic parodies as he follows a watery way to vulgarity and stupidity, while Céladon is borne off by the currents to ladies of the highest culture.

On another level, though, Francion's schoolboy poverty adventures in Paris are about to be repeated: once again, he is on his own without financial resources in a world which understands only appearances. This time, however, as a kind of demonstration of his learning process, he chooses to enjoy his fate and to exploit this new imposed disguise in a manner somewhat reminiscent of Clérante's behavior during the peasant marriage masquerade (F, 270-89). Francion utilizes his new situation as protection from dishonor. The world of the peasantry is now open to him, and he can deflower its virgins without shame because, following the lesson of *paraître*, he is what he appears to be.[7] And so, by utilization of a very cynical rationale which exploits the prejudice of the ignorant, he can have any peasant woman without regret or reprisal.

Hence, the masquerade illustrates a kind of learning process. Francion, deprived of financial resources, understands his limitations and makes the best of his situation without expressing the bitter indignation which poverty caused him as a youth. Instead, he joyfully exploits another milieu by mystifying its inhabitants with feats of magic and by gratifying his sexual whims. Of course, Francion eventually escapes from this bucolic world and works his way back to France, where he is able to reassume his former social status. But all along the way, he exults in his cleverness in surviving at a lower rank. In a sense, this episode is almost the converse of his youthful adventures, for it confirms the preeminence of quality even when unperceived. When the iron-clad restrictions of *paraître* are not exceeded, the person of quality may make the best of things and revel in a potentially depressing situation.

The Joconde seduction occurs as a postscript to Francion's adventures as a shepherd and constitutes a magnificent play on appearances. The hero, still in peasant garb, listens to Joconde's complaints about the lack of realism in pastorals: peasants with refined speech irritate her (F, 381). He then reveals to this realistic maiden that there are in the area men dressed as peasants who are "capables de faire l'amour avec autant de civilité, de prudence, et de discretion que les personnes qui sont dans la plus florissante Cour de la terre" (F, 382). The surprise of this avowal and Francion's obvious refinement lead to Joconde's inevitable seduction. In a sense, this adventure functions as the converse of Francion's problems in the courtship of Diane (F, 223). Impoverished, he had to await his mother's dole before he could afford to dress for the part of Diane's suitor. And so this amusing seduction creates an extended juxtaposition with the problems of a younger, less able Francion and offers one more proof that he has definitely reached the height of his skills. But this adventure, clearly another sarcastic jab at the pastoral, also functions as an exception to the exigencies of *paraître* which proves the rule. Francion has exploited a shocking aberration from the laws of appearance. This is a one-of-a-kind seductive situation, a clever insider's joke which comically affirms the reborn hero's intrinsic superiority.

Francion's pastoral adventures come to an end when his tryst with Joconde is interrupted by a minor social upheaval. He is injured in an attempt to flee her quarters. Barely able to walk and incriminatingly close to Joconde's residence, he sits down in a sedan chair just vacated by its former occupant, the seditious *vieillard goutteux*. He is carried to the governor's palace, and, a victim of mistaken identity, he finds himself haughtily interrogated as a criminal. After comic replies to the governor's misdirected queries, Francion is finally released.

What is the importance of this apparently extraneous episode? First of all, this adventure immediately precedes Francion's resolution to return to Lyons, to re-equip himself for a new quest for Nays, and, in particular, to exchange his shepherd's costume for a new disguise. The disguises of both the orgy and the shepherd episode were accompanied by suggestions of death—Raymond's threat of execution and the boat-bier. Once again this menace occurs. This time, however, it is the reader rather than the hero who is aware of imminent danger. Francion, blissfully uninformed of the governor's intention to execute him, treats the latter's threats as jokes and replies humorously. Closer examination would suggest that this situation effects a reversal of Francion's attitude at the beginning of the orgy. In both cases, he is an invalid at the mercy of a powerful lord, and, in both cases, the grounds for the death threat are insignificant. In a sense, Francion's reaction may embody a form of progress towards lucidity. He is no longer intimidated by absurd death threats. He does not panic at the governor's rage. His confidence and self-assurance free him from irrational fears; after all, he is totally innocent. In these episodes the structural antitheses move from negative to positive in order to eliminate useless anguish. The reiteration of situations, all under the aegis of disguise, is employed to express change and improvement in the principal character.[8]

Shortly before his arrival in Lyons, still dressed in the soldier's clothes, Francion is mistaken for a quack by the local peasantry. Unable to resist a new prank, he mystifies the villagers with his medicines and prophecy. This final masquerade reiterates the exploitation of the peasantry and reaffirms Francion's role as a relatively unscrupulous manipulator of the ignorant. It is another demonstration of his skills at surviving in adversity.

Francion's disguises clearly realize multiple functions. Besides depicting his growth as the hero, they enable him to play the trickster, to step out of an otherwise constraining role, and to enter the world of the lower classes. In one sense, these disguises are a seventeenth-century device for creating social breadth. On the other hand, they insulate by permitting contact without contamination.

Polyandre

Polyandre does not disguise himself nearly so frequently as Francion or Lysis—in fact, he disguises himself only once, as Frère Polycarpe. The use of disguise is, on the whole, very infrequent in this novel, and this restriction of the novel's scope may be part of a general attempt to make the *Polyandre* into a comedy of manners, i.e., more realistic. Despite its diminution, the principal function of disguise remains the same for Polyandre as for Francion: to manifest the hero's superiority over the ignorant and to share his scornful attitude with his peers. Polyandre demonstrates this use of costume when, disguised as Frère Polycarpe, he deceives the opinionated Mme Ragonde, a veritable bourgeois ogress.[9]

This aged creature comes to Aurélie's salon to lecture her daughter and granddaughters about propriety and to remind these successful parvenues of their humble origins, of which she is a dreadful and embarrassing relic. Sorel uses the person of Mme Ragonde to assail certain bourgeois convictions: not the values of the upwardly mobile *nouveaux riches*, the *noblesse de robe*, but those of their grandparents, who remained too brutally financial, too morally straight-jacketed, and too rigidly limited to their own class. Unlike the *Francion*, in which Sorel, superficially at least, seems to resent any effort at bourgeois ascension, by attacking Ragonde he now takes the side of those of his class who are successfully penetrating into the nobility and discarding the stodgy lifestyle which characterized the bourgeois condition.

At an appropriate pause in Ragonde's diatribe against the corruption of the century, Polyandre appears disguised as Frère Polycarpe. His description is clearly a forerunner of Molière's Tartuffe:

Ayant un habit noir de drap de Hollande sans aucune dentelle, il estoit fort propre à contrefaire un homme modeste & un contempteur des vanitez du Monde: Premierement il avoit réhaussé ses bottes iusques par dessus le genouïl, cachant ses éguilletes & ses bas à botter, comme des ornemens superflus; Apres il avoit mis son collet en dedans si avant qu'il ne luy restoit qu'un poulce aux dehors; Puis ayant tiré de sa posche une callotte de marroquin qu'il mettoit quelquefois lors qu'il estoit enrheumé, où lors qu'il estoit obligé de se tenir long temps découvert quelque part, il avoit res-serré presque tous ses cheveux au dessous, & ayant aussi rabaissé sa moustache, il ressembloit à quelque Frere Oblat qui venoit de la campagne. (P, II, 336-37)

Though disguise episodes for the hero are limited to one in the *Polyandre*, this particular episode is, nevertheless, more lavishly detailed in its description than many in Sorel's works. Sorel seems to be striving for a more literal form of realism, leaving almost nothing to the reader's imagination. The extreme detail about Polyandre's costuming is surely necessary as a counter-point to the elaborate physical description of Mme Ragonde, which I have supplied in n. 9, but it is also motivated by an attempt to be more vivid and hence more comical. The novel itself seems to be moving towards the theatrical, with descrip-tions that could be costuming instructions.

Upon his appearance, Polyandre feigns the piety of *l'homme dévot* to the enormous pleasure of the susceptible Mme Ragonde. His objectives are twofold: to tame this fury by transforming her into an object of amusement for a group of privileged spec-tators and at the same time to impress Aurélie with his wit and humor, thus furthering his amorous designs. As regards the per-son of the dupe, there has been an obvious shift of focus: the peasantry has been replaced by a monster of the bourgeoisie. Consistent with the realism of the description, Sorel seems to be trying to bring his satire closer to home, to characters more immediate in the life of his Parisian readers. While there are situ-ations in the *Francion* and the *Berger* in which characters try to impress their lovers by exploiting a dupe in a disguise episode, the episodes have as targets characters somewhat removed from daily life: an outlandish pedant and a novel-crazed youth.[10] But in the *Polyandre*, a novel that has been supposedly "deliber-tinized," Sorel's alleged conservatism gives way to a caustic par-ody of the contemporary abuses of piety. One wonders just how much of the youthful Sorel persisted and whether he had simply become more guarded rather than repentant. His keen sense of the abuse of appearances led him to attack the new religious hypocrisy as depicted in Frère Polycarpe. He did not hesitate to suggest that Polycarpe's pious observations were worthy only of the consideration of senile curmudgeons. In a restrained sense, his libertinism lives on in this courageous indictment of religious fraud. The Frère Polycarpe masquerade, then, fulfills many purposes. It enhances Polyandre's standing with Aurélie by turning the noisome Ragonde into an object of amusement, and it confirms the general role of Sorel's heroes in disguise, that of the successful trickster. But most importantly, it opens up a new area of social satire.[11]

## Lysis and His "Friends"

If the Frère Polycarpe episode is a demonstration of Polyandre's living up to his epithet, "l'adroict," Lysis' several disguises are clearly devastating attacks on the pastoral and heroic novels. Omitting his transformation into a tree, Lysis puts on three disguises: the principal is his shepherd's costume, mark of his folly and worn regularly throughout the novel; the second is the transvestite apparel of the Amarylle adventure; and the last, the rather tatty classical garb which he dons for an "heroic" mission. Sorel's opening description of Lysis' shepherd attire is filled with sarcastic comments which indicate that Lysis is a bit too fashionable to be the typical wretched peasant of the *Francion*. In fact, Sorel insists upon its theatricality and thus clearly differentiates Lysis from the bestial creatures so typical in the comic novels.[12] Lysis is a player whose costume's peculiarity will be evidence of his inauthenticity. The very absurdity of his finery touches the heart of the pastoral, striking at its lack of realism, its "shepherds of quality." While Francion uses shepherd's garb as a kind of shield, an escape from ordinary social constraints, and as a means to exploit his inferiors, Lysis' clothing, donned by preference, serves as the outward sign of his own unwitting derogation.

The Amarylle adventure once again focuses pointedly upon the pastoral by bringing out the absurdity of transvestite adventures, stock sequences in contemporary novels. Lysis, of course, justifies his behavior by citing all the principal transvestite episodes he has culled from his wide readings. Obvious factors, such as gender errors when he refers to himself and his inability even to deceive an old peasant woman in his disguise as the maidservant Amarylle, give Lysis away immediately and thus signal the artificiality of such travesties. Indignation with the abuse of verisimilitude seems always to spur Sorel on to unabating, destructive mockery. His intolerance for the preposterous rationalizations which his contemporaries used to make these episodes credible was absolute. The modern reader often feels that Sorel is beating a dead horse, yet, given the frequency of such episodes in *L'Astrée* and the massive cultural predilection for such adventures in the seventeenth century, one must wonder if the imbalance we perceive in Sorel's attacks today does not stem from a relative absence of such episodes in contemporary literature. Indeed, for those who were exasperated by novels filled with young men running about in dresses, living interminably as women, Sorel's virulent and caustic mockery might well have appeared balanced and judicious.

Lysis' masquerade as a classical hero is not designed to fool anyone. Rather, it should represent his apotheosis, for it marks the beginning of his mission to deliver Méliante's imprisoned mistress. The whole episode is, of course, a practical joke. Here one may assume that Sorel is making reference to the *Francion*, for this episode clearly calls to mind Francion's classical garb at the libertine orgy. But the latter's attire, however ambivalent (Francion believes that he is to be a sacrificial victim), suggests a noble pomp: "l'on luy mit allentour du col une chaisne de diamants, et un chappeau sur la teste, dont le cordon estoit encore de pierreries d'une extreme valeur" (F, 306). As I have remarked, he will in this costume proclaim his doctrine of free love. Since all the other libertines join him by donning similar attire, the elite adopts a sort of uniform. Costume serves to enhance the truth rather than hide it. In short, all the normal functions of disguise will be suspended to indicate a privileged moment. Lysis' disguise, quite predictably, has a completely opposite function. His costume is makeshift and ignoble (BE, 369), and it designates his efforts as mock heroic. Here Sorel insists that the past cannot be recaptured,[13] and he denies Lysis the link with the classical heritage which he so willingly granted to Francion.

It is not Lysis, but rather Anselme, Hircan, and the others, who use costume in the manner of Francion and Polyandre. Their disguises as river gods and those of their various lady friends who become nymphs have only one function: the nurturing of Lysis' follies. The situation of the *Francion* is clearly turned inside out with the principal character cast in the role of fool. The pattern of a disguised hero striking out at many targets is reversed, and everything is concentrated on a central character instead of a plurality of fools and villains. Nevertheless, the result is really the same. While there is no hero to exalt, a homogeneous series of targets is set up in the name of realism. In the *Francion*, the disguised hero attacks ignorance, represented principally by the credulous and superstitious, such as Valentin and the peasantry, or by vain and pretentious people, illustrated chiefly by Hortensius. In fact, the groundwork of the anti-pastoral was already laid in the *Francion*, which offers a more grotesque vision of the conditions of the peasantry than the *Berger*. In the latter, the attack focuses more precisely on the forms of literature itself, and thus the preoccupation is less to describe the actual condition of the peasantry than to effect an episode-by-episode demolition of the pastoral. But in both cases, it is the cause of realism which is being served. The *Francion*, through its vigorous and youthful hero, preaches a general lucidity, whereas the *Berger* elaborates the harmful effects of a particular form of cultivated illusion. The disguised hero of the *Polyandre* has the same ultimate aim as the hero of the *Francion*, but here the satire has been transferred to the very salons of Paris. Disguise, then, equally characterizes the hero in the role of privileged observer and the anti-hero in that of dupe. But whatever the role of the masquerader, the basic function of disguise episodes remains consistent: chastening ignorant foibles and upholding commonsensical realism.

The Monomaniacs

The most important of the monomaniacs in the *Francion* is Hortensius, and it is hardly surprising that his disguises serve as models for those of the others. Basically, this avaricious school-master is always in disguise because he is a peasant; even as a teacher he has exceeded his station. His two masquerade epi-sodes—the boots story, deliberately contrived by Hortensius, and the King of Poland episode, concocted by Francion and his entourage—illustrate two separate models of masquerade which run through the monomaniac disguise sections of the other novels.

The boots story is really part of a topos in which the most symbolic aspect of the monomaniac's clothing will turn against him and ironically become a source of injury rather than social elevation. Hortensius' adventure was already prepared in *La Louange et l'utilité des bottes*. [14] As the author mockingly suggests, boots offer a wonderful way to pass for a gentleman: "Mais si l'on veut passer plus avant, n'est-ce pas un grand avan-tage que de paroistre Chevalier estant botté, encore que l'on n'ayt point de cheval, d'autant que ceux qui vous voyent s'imagi-nent que vostre monture n'est pas loin." [15] Hortensius' dilemma is anticipated in this pamphlet when it relates the woes of a "Gentilhomme" accused of killing a child in a riding accident. [16] The booted Hortensius is taken to court on the same accusation. To save himself, he makes a humiliating public denial of his equestrian abilities: he admits to never having ridden more than a donkey. A similar system operates in the Frémonde episode, when Hortensius comes wearing a sword—another indicator of noble status—to make marriage arrangements with that woman. Once his true background as a swineherd is revealed, the func-tion of the disguise is reversed and the sword becomes evidence of fraud. By the rules of this topos, costume cannot serve the interests of the monomaniac, but rather it leads to public sham-ing. The monomaniac may never deceive; he can only embarrass himself in the attempt.

The same mechanisms apply to the story of Musigène's golden braid (*cordon*). He is arrested by the "Sergens" for wearing this decoration in violation of the king's edict; however, upon inves-tigation, the offending braid turns out to be dyed straw (P, I, 398). Musigène's vanity is publicly unmasked: he is, after all, a rag-tag poet obsessed by a kind of seventeenth-century dandyism. But the "Sergens" are also humiliated by the crowd, and Musigène himself is subject to mixed treatment: both sympathy and mockery. As I remarked earlier, Sorel moderates his treatment of the monomaniacs in the *Polyandre*. The same obtains for Orilan. He sports a red wig as a symbol of his flaming passion. But it is hoisted from his head as a practical joke at the ball. Like Musigène he becomes an object of both amusement and sympathy: by the merriment his discomfiture provokes and through the admiration he excites in handling a difficult situation with wit and grace. In other words, the topos initiated in *La Louange* endures, but with greater moderation of its humiliation mechanism in regard to the monomaniacs. Only in the case of the scoundrel Héliodore does the object have the same damning effect as with Hortensius. An alembic is caught over his head as he flees a group of enraged townspeople, the former dupes of his alchemy. Here it is the equipment, not the actual clothing itself, which serves as the key object in indicating the monomaniac's fraud or social pretension, but, on the whole, Sorel's technique offers very slight variation from his earliest to his later comic works.

Hortensius' other masquerade—the King of Poland episode—sets the pattern for the *Berger* in that the other characters nurture the illusion of the monomaniac by pretending to accept his costume as reality. In Hortensius' case, the aim is to drive him mad. Disguise thus deprived of its principal purpose—to deceive others—turns inward on its wearer to his total undoing: Hortensius is doomed to await eternally the return of the vanished "Polish ambassadors" who offered him the throne and provoked his ridiculous masquerade. The *paraître* is never at the monomaniac's disposal, because by definition he is too limited to exploit it for his own ends.

Clearly this last kind of masquerade—Hortensius' most extravagant and the only form Lysis knows—is the most anti-literary. In every instance in the *Berger*, it is used to ridicule some contemporary genre. In the *Francion*, the King of Poland episode is preceded by Hortensius bragging about his authorial prowess; later on in the episode, he comes to believe in his own kingly status because of the many cases of fictional characters who suddenly discover their noble origins. The more Hortensius relies on literature, the more he abuses his own reason. Sorel thus reserved the most preposterous form of masquerade for his most hated target: the contemporary novel.

## Language and the Art of Dissimulation

The successfully manipulative characters of Sorel's comic novels all lie with abandon, and, in that sense, their language follows a pattern that is quite parallel to disguise. But beyond this obvious observation, there is ample room for specific commentary on their language and that of the monomaniacs, as a manifestation of successful or unsuccessful dissimulation, as a structure which reflects each character's function, or even his "essence." In fact, this comparison of language and disguise quite naturally refers back to the distinction made between heroes and monomaniacs in ch. 2. For the sake of clarity, we shall first examine language as used by successful players and then turn to language as used by their victims.

Three of Francion's numerous masquerades are particularly interesting as instances of disguise enhanced by language: the peasant marriage episode, the pastoral interlude, and the charlatan masquerade. In the first, Francion and Clérante, disguised as itinerant musicians, offer colorful examples of the use of patois, for they carry on briefly in a kind of country jargon during the festivities. Francion's joking includes expressions like "vertu goy," and the general drift of his conversation is towards obscene equivocation which compares woman first to a violin and then to a flute. Several aspects of successful manipulation are manifest. Most importantly, Francion grasps the level of his interlocutors and uses a language which suits their milieu. This further implies a kind of ironic doubling of the trickster, for he must understand the separation of his real person from that of the character he adopts. His words and phrasing must be as accurate as the details of the costume he dons. Secondly, his language, even on this level, must manifest his superiority. Francion's ability to draw an analogy and then sustain his double entendre serves as a demonstration of intellectual force or, put quite simply, control of the situation. He must also maintain the correct tone—in this case, coarsely erotic—by using the proper linguistic register. Finally, he must succeed in his operation—here the seduction of the Bourgeoise by Clérante. Of course, both characters play their roles admirably, and Clérante's pseudo-drunken boasting exalting his genital endowments does have the desired effect on the Bourgeoise, who has already been predisposed to lechery by Francion's insinuations, not to mention her own lustfulness. The episode, in brief, is a clear instance of disguise and language working in a perfect mimetic coordination.

Francion's "musical" seduction during the mock pastoral episode in Italy also relies heavily on equivocation:

Alors elle [a young peasant girl] s'assist proche de luy, et l'ayant prié de luy monstrer son instrument et d'en joüer, il luy dit ainsi: Ma bonne amie, jamais vous ne vistes chose si miraculeuse que ce que je fay pour produire ma melodie. Pour ne vous rien celer, j'ay point d'instrument qui soit fait de bois ny de corne. L'harmonie ne provient que des membres de mon corps qui la produisent tous ensemble. La fille s'imagina alors qu'en faisant certaines postures, et en se remuant de quelque sorte, il avoit l'industrie de faire craqueter ses os, si bien qu'ils rendoient quelque son, ou bien qu'il frappoit de ses mains sur ses membres pour les faire claquer. Mais elle apprit bien tost qu'il y avoit bien encore autre chose a faire. (F, 368-69)

Here there is no emphasis on the change of linguistic register. But this equivocation is, nevertheless, completely in keeping with the spirit of the peasant masquerade: totally outrageous, unabashedly sexual, almost predatory. Once again, Francion has correctly grasped the level of his interlocutor, who listens with enraptured curiosity. There is the appropriate communication between the actor, who maintains an ironic distance thanks to his convenient persona, and a victim, who accepts his words as surely as she accepts his shepherd's garments. Language becomes another form of power. Here words place the ignorant at the mercy of their betters. These double entendres are Francion's *tour de force*, revealing him as a master of language by his very ability to disguise the meaning of his utterances and as a master of debauchery in his skill at deflowering yet another virgin.

In Francion's final disguise scene in the novel, he plays the role of a charlatan and offers a last example of language and costuming coinciding to create the desired effect. The problem of communication lies in the necessity to convey to a group of villagers who have mistaken him for a charlatan that he has curative and prophetic powers. Quickly adopting the correct register, Francion assumes the brash tones, the bragadoccio of a medicine hawker and thus, through language, continues the impression that his vaguely soldierly costume has made on the villagers. Again, there is a perfect correspondence between his intentions and his results: he persuades the peasants to buy his medicine and even makes an absurd prophecy. In short, bluster begets bluster in a semantic outpouring of preposterous claims.

In the case of Lysis' various companions, communication is between a series of clear-sighted players and a somewhat deranged victim who fails to realize the doubling he is practicing. Their objective is to continue the mystification of one individual or to collaborate in his auto-mystification. Their language must thus aim at one overall register: the literary. It is not an issue of adopting patois or taking on a huckster's tone and vocabulary, but rather of choosing the appropriate style within the wide scope of contemporary literature. Language instantly becomes extended parody, and its efficacy is measured by Lysis' all-too-willing acceptance. The novel abounds in examples—in fact, it is largely composed of them. We can briefly refer to Hircan, who, the moment Lysis mistakes him for a magician, advances outlandish claims of magical power in a grandiloquent literary style (BE, 151). The many escapades of this domineering personnage constitute amplifications of this trait: for instance, his magical incantation which restores humanity to Lysis "the tree." All the characters study novels in order to play these roles, to be assured, among other things, of the appropriate diction and tone. The two wandering Persian shepherds, Méliante and Polidor, are perfect examples of this, for they combine playacting with tales replete with the most absurd metaphors and successfully deceive the receptive Lysis with outrageous parodies of the novel of adventure. This permanent literary register of the *Berger* is taken to its logical extreme when all the characters, including Lysis, put on theater performances and when, for once, even the crazed shepherd engages in a conscious parody of language. The chief difference between the use of language as disguise by manipulators in the *Berger* and in the *Francion* is that the tricksters of the former use a language that would immediately fail in the latter. The reason is clear: it is because of the exclusive target of the *Berger*, the naïve Lysis.

In the *Polyandre*, the hero or manipulator, though he does not scruple to bend the truth when it becomes advantageous to do so, dons only one disguise: that of Frère Polycarpe. He does so with a perfect awareness of his audience, which is actually double: Mme Ragonde, the victim, and the rest of the party at Aurélie's, the delighted spectators. To deceive the old woman and to entertain the others, Polyandre must deftly manipulate the register of contemporary piety. Accordingly, his language literally oozes false humility and, occasionally, righteous anger. Polyandre presents himself as "le pauvre frere Polycape à vostre service . . . le moindre de tous qui cherchent la voye de salut" (P, II, 339). His language is richly seasoned with sententious platitudes: "La retraite du corps, Madame . . . est la felicité de l'ame" (ibid.). We know that Polyandre's mimesis is perfect because Mme Ragonde confirms it by her reaction, itself an accurate description of his discourse: "Tout ce qu'il dit n'est que sentences & paroles dorées" (P, II, 341). He goes on to advance his occupation as a reformer of other people's lives, giving himself a Tartuffe-like role, and refers to his "sainte colère" at immoral living. In a curious sense, Polyandre has lived up to his name—"Un homme . . . qui est propre à beaucoup de choses, & mesme à tout faire" (P, I, ã iii)—for he has demonstrated a protean adaptability. In this respect, his language confers upon him a power exactly analogous to that of Francion, the master of metamorphosis.

In short, Sorelian manipulators move through language with the same facility as they adopt costumes. The world at large does not perceive the radical disjunction between sign and meaning. Instead, their doubling remains a secret carefully guarded from their victims, with whom they enjoy ironic relationships. Sorelian manipulators are masters of both verbal and physical surfaces, and the differing relationships they enjoy with the monomaniacs are expressed at the physical and semantic levels by disguise and lies. Language thus becomes another aspect of their formal or external multiplicity which furthers their adoption of convenient personae.

Like the manipulators, the anti-hero and the monomaniacs also strive to make their words correspond to disguise: to use them as a manner of adopting another condition. But since they use them in an attempt to transcend their low status, they inevitably achieve the diametrical opposite of what they seek in the *Francion* and the *Berger*; and, to a lesser extent, they follow the same course in the *Polyandre*, where their objectives have been modified. When language, as it were, descends to the occasion, the monomaniacs will often speek in *galimatias*, a term which Sorel defines in reference to the theater character Jason, played by Lysis:

Son langage est celuy des Courtisans qui n'ont pas estudié & qui se pensent faire admirer par des discours où personne ne peut rien entendre, lesquels ils ont pris dans des livres d'amour. Ce nom de galimatias n'a point d'origine certaine, & toutefois l'on en use maintenant dans les serieux livres pour signifier le langage que je dy: mais le premier qui a usé de ce mot est le Comedien Bruscambille, qui l'a donné pour tiltre à quelques uns de ses Prologues qui ont esté faits pour n'avoir point de sens. (BE, "Remarques," p. 660)

Clearly, the emphasis is placed on the ignorance of the speaker and the unintelligibility of his discourse. In a sense, *galimatias* is the perfect tool for Sorel because it permits him to strike out at his favorite topic—the abuse of words—and thus to promote his notion of realism, which, as we have seen, is so closely tied to language correctly or appropriately used.

But it is especially fascinating to consider *galimatias* as a kind of verbal costume which the monomaniac assumes when he wishes to make a particular impression. By dressing up his vocabulary, Hortensius tries to present himself as a literate lover, as a great wielder of words. He speaks in tirades that are merely an accumulation of praise or invective as the case may be. In courting Frémonde, he sends the following "billet doux":

. . . et ma volonté y recevant l'idole de vos monstrueuses beautez, y faict grandement les honneurs de la maison: vous aurez donc tousjours a ceste cause l'image de mes affections au devant de vos yeux, et mettrez vostre nez dedans afin de voir comme elles sont innumerables. Arrachez les vostres de vostre cœur pour me reciproquer, s'il vous plaist, et n'affligez plus mon repos comme vous avez fait par cy devant. (F, 191-92)

The most obvious problem with this love letter, which precedes Hortensius' disguise as a nobleman, is that it is a failure of communication. Hortensius envisions himself as an elegant and urbane suitor, whereas he is no more than a clown to Frémonde. It is obvious that he has not understood the essentials of romantic discourse and that he sees this inflated vocabulary as a sign which corresponds to an altogether different meaning than the one assigned to it by the reader of the letter. Like his sword, his words, which may be richly valued in isolation, do not, when inserted into discourse, achieve the desired effect. They are proofs of his incompetence, just as the sword is shameful evidence of his imposture. His discourse in mimetically inept and thus without true referentiality. A closer analysis of his writing reveals that Hortensius has brutalized his metaphor—"l'image de mes affections"—by interpreting it literally: he maintains that Frémonde will stick her nose into it. He is also guilty of a clumsy, contradictory wording when he coins the unwitting oxymoron, "monstrueuses beautez." This bumbling shows that he is incapable of sustaining a noble style. His inherent baseness is transparent, just as it is when he is in disguise. In fact, his communication is punctuated by common expressions and clichés (putting one's nose into things, troubling his rest) and by a barbarous abuse of noble language ("Arrachez les vostres de vostre cœur"). His entire discourse betrays an incapacity to attain an ironic perspective on himself. Just as when he is in costume, he forgets who he really is and assumes that, by taking on another language form, he is in fact another, whereas he is hopelessly mired in his own system of referentiality. And so his language runs amuck along a spiraling course of whacky and aberrant semantic associations. From word to word, clause to clause, his utterances turn on each other in a form of contradiction which manifests a complete dichotomy between intention and effect. His language becomes a failed assimilation of another condition which condemns in one stroke the lofty diatribes of novels and Hortensius' own pretensions to social ascension.

In the previous chapter, we discussed the differences between the monomaniacs and the madman Collinet. At this juncture, it would be helpful to show how, despite Collinet's use of *galima-*

*tias*, he never seems to create the same effect as Hortensius. The destination and objectives of his discourse probably have much to do with this. Each *galimatias* is normally provoked as a form of entertainment: he is given a chair to hold forth before Luce. In this *galimatias*, his discourse seems incomprehensible, full of changes of register from the lofty to the base, loaded with common expressions, full of semantic spiraling, usually obscene, and apparently exclusively intrareferential. But Collinet's discourses are inevitably well received. His words are awaited by Luce and they are given the jester's liberty. He is also recognized as insane, with no particular ambition or desire to transcend his condition. Because he can be prophetic—Luce's seduction—his utterances assume a certain communicative value despite their superficially hermetic aspect. In short, his linguistic universe intersects that of the monomaniacs, but does not really coincide with it. The context delivers him from the cycle of failure and pretension that is their lot.

Lysis' diatribes, though considerably more lucid and controlled than either Hortensius' or Collinet's, are to some extent a form of modified *galimatias*. This is especially true when he addresses the shepherd and the hermit, for neither can understand his florid, richly metaphorical language. What is critical, however, is Lysis' belief that by adopting the language of the pastoral he actually becomes a shepherd. Again, his linguistic disguise can fool no one: language fails to conceal his true identity, just as his shepherd's garments were entirely too fancy to allow him to pass for a person of that condition.

When Lysis himself consciously uses *galimatias* in playing the role of Jason, he also portrays someone trying to be what he is not: a courtier adept in the vocabulary of love rather than a warrior:

Belle ame de mon ame, desir de mon desir, sejour de mes conceptions, ne faut-il pas que vous croyez que ma franchise s'est immolée sur l'Autel de vos beautez? Depuis que je vous connoy je suis merveilleusement amoureux d'une si amoureuse merveille, & je ne cherche plus qu'a mourir pour vous d'une vivante mort qui vale mieux qu'une mourante vie. (BE, 363)

This example of *galimatias* demonstrates in a more refined fashion than in Hortensius' letter that the language of love is fraudulence itself, because Jason's ridiculous contortions of language implicitly condemn passionate hyperbole. His utterances represent language gone astray, analogous to items of attire misused. In *galimatias*, language does not communicate, but rather it mimicks itself, just as Lysis' shepherd's garments and his hero's costume grotesquely imitate an unattainable model. This kind of *galimatias* conceals Sorel's plea for a more rational use of words and also betrays a certain fascination with the mechanics of discourse. Again, this corresponds to his implicit and explicit critique of judgments based on a person's clothing and his wry amusement at playing with various articles of attire, at making them ape another social condition.

Even when Lysis' habitual language is not strictly *galimatias*, it still illustrates the various defects of monomaniacal communication and role-playing. His love letter to Charite may be taken as an example:

L'Amour ayant pris vos beautez pour armes, avoit dés long temps assiegé ma liberté, qui s'estoit retiree dans le fort de ma raison, lors que sans se servir d'escalade, il est volé dedans mes yeux, & est entré par là iusques dans mon ame comme un voleur entre dans une maison par les fenestres. Les maux qu'il m'a fait souffrir sont fort violens, mais enfin estant adoucy, il m'a iuré que vous y pourriez donner du remede, & qu'il ne tenoit à autre chose qu'à vous en escrire. Voyant alors que i'estois un Escrivain fort mal fourny des outils de mon mestier, il a tiré une plume de son aisle, & me l'a taillee avec la pointe de son dard; il m'a donné du papier qui avoit esté fait avec ses vieux bandeaux, par un Papetier celeste. Il a pris des charbons de mon cœur qui est à moictié bruslé, & les ayant escachez il les a destrempez avec mes larmes, & m'en a fait de l'ancre. C'est avec cecy que i'ay escrit, & pour seicher les lettres, il a ietté dessus des cendres qu'il a prises au mesme lieu que les charbons . . . . (BE, 82)

Once again, the context is inappropriate and the communicative nature of Lysis' letter is doomed from the onset. Charite, ignorant as she is, could never understand the missive. The letter is constructed upon a spiriling of metaphors based on an overliteralized semantic association: Cupid's wings, his feathers, and the coals from Lysis' heart are all used in a perversely logical development. But this amplification is too literal and thus becomes foolish; it automatically banalizes metaphorical power. In a sense, this corresponds to Lysis' overdone costuming. Reality is entirely banished by metaphorical hypertrophy. Further, Lysis does not appropriately manipulate his registers: Love's entrance as a robber coming through his eyes as through the house windows spoils the romantic tone. To make matters worse, the whole action of the poem is logically impossible: Anselme points out that the letter could not be dried until it was folded. Sorel underscores the weakness of this "poetic" prolepsis and even uses it as a critique of Marot (BE, "Remarques," p. 574). Lysis' letter is thus another form of literary parody, like disguise, for it marks contemporary love letters as pretentious, affected, absurd, and, worse, illogical.

The monomaniacs of the *Polyandre* also use a language that departs radically from normal communication, although it generally remains intelligible, for, just as disguise is restricted in this novel, so, to some degree, is linguistic outrageousness. Musigène, Orilan, Gastrimargue and Théophraste (Héliodore) all take their liberties with expression, warping it to their own particular self-images. Naturally, Gastrimargue's is the most pretentious and the most inappropriate. Polyandre himself provides a most interesting analysis of Gastrimargue's language as failed projection. The hero realizes that Gastrimargue's vocabulary and expressions are meant to impress: to convey a notion of learning and eloquence, to foster the pedant's unsuccessful persona as a great scholar. Polyandre, nevertheless, characterizes Gastrimargue's language as a limited stock of phrases for all occasions, or, in an uncharitable assessment of those who are impressed by it, as "un bast pour les asnes" (P, II, 414). Gastrimargue's speech lacks imagination, his favorite form being anagrams—a simple form which corresponds to a simple mind. His verses are irregular (incompetent by contemporary standards) and their meaning obscure. His grotesque figures are fit only for almanachs and his discourse is clumsy plagiarism. In short, Gastrimargue's language is inappropriate to the image that he wishes to convey, inadequately mimetic. His utterances are marked by the characteristic rupture between sign and signified. In fact, this synopsis of Gastrimargue's verbal flaws could be generalized to all monomaniac discourse, which is precisely a failure to achieve an effective referentiality, a failure that stems from the monomaniac's incapacity to appreciate the distance between his person and his persona. Since Gastrimargue refuses to acknowledge his real person, language, like disguise, can only constitute a form of wish fulfillment.

The same obtains for the charlatan Théophraste. His assertions about his profound knowledge of alchemy and his pretensions to magical abilities are instantly seen through by the more lucid characters. Like the monomaniacs of a literary bent, he uses a vast array of learned terms, only his are more "scientific." Like the others, his utterances are mimetically deficient, and he relies on a discourse of expansion based on semi-learned terminology and on flatly ignorant assertions which beget yet more preposterous claims. Largely unsuccessful, he fails to persuade Mélinte's father to invest in his alchemy and shortly afterwards undergoes a public disgrace. Later on, he encounters a similar skepticism from M. Péralde. His incompetence at hucksterism is constantly seconded by his obvious venality, if not outright mendacity. In short, poorly dressed and chronically needy, Théophraste's external appearance and financial condition always correspond to the shoddy verbal impression he makes on the perceptive. His vocabulary is incapable of engendering the persuasive force needed to create a convincing persona.

Though Musigène and Orilan escape more lightly than the others, their verbal exchanges also exhibit many of Gastrimargue's and Théophraste's flaws. Both characters do not create the impressions they wish to convey. At the beginning of the novel, despite his various attempts to patch up his deteriorating clothing, Musigène inevitably figures as a *poète crottesque* rather than the elegant man of letters he wishes to represent. His words, on this occasion and others, show the same futile striving for effect. For instance, in an unrestrained hyperbole, he maintains that one act of the play he is working on would require the felling of an entire forest just to provide the machinery for the stage sets. This blatant exaggeration parallels his dress, and it clearly belies his claims to authorial imagination. Likewise, his grandiose words to the portrait merely cast him as an ineffectual buffoon—an effect that is reinforced when the portrait is brutally snatched from his grasp. Both Musigène and Orilan try to convince Néophile of the superiority of their approaches to love. Again, it is a shower of preposterous claims. Musigène extols the wealth of poetic forms which one must use to become an accomplished suitor. The excess of this panegyric undermines the alleged benefits of poetry. Likewise, Orilan's policy of playing the universal lover is described in such far-fetched terms (he has even received proposals from oriental princesses!), with such a plethora of extraordinary benefits, that it becomes self-discrediting, nothing more than a paean to his eccentricity. Indeed, Néophile listens to none of them in his pursuit of Aurélie. Their inflated utterances merely become language for the sake of language, and Musigène and Orilan lose sight of the true purpose of words: to communicate effectively, to exchange ideas, and to influence. They become trapped in a web of imperfect mimesis, which automatically restricts them to the role of entertainers rather than influencers.

Yet their communications are decidedly more effective than Gastrimargue's or Théophraste's. Musigène and Orilan are the habitués of worldly salons, and they realize that their job is to entertain through preposterous conversation. In a way, they fulfill a function previously assigned to Collinet, but they do so quite lucidly. Accordingly, Orilan's witticisms at the financier's ball become a subject of admiration: he does have quick retorts and a fertile imagination to justify his peculiar manner of courting. Musigène, as has been remarked, is a lively story-teller when he is given the chance to ridicule his enemy Gastrimargue. Both Musigène and Orilan entertain the guests at Aurélie's salon with their badinage: they manage a sustained metaphorical combat based on eyes as suns and, as previously mentioned, have a very literary debate on Orilan's courting behavior as opposed to that of Lysis, in the *Berger*, and Hylas, in *L'Astrée*. In fact, Orilan even emerges from this comparison triumphantly superior. In short, the conscious humor which pervades the language of Orilan and Musigène separates their discourse from the contemptible utterances of Gastrimargue and the knavery of Théophraste. In their case, language is not only a questionable attempt to overcome a lowly station, but also a form of entertainment at which they have a genuine, though limited, proficiency.

Thus, language, like disguise, can be measured by its efficacy in creating a persona. For a hero or manipulator, it readily accommodates itself to his purpose; all his utterances are skill-fully delivered at the appropriate register, and the disjunction between sign and signified is effectively obscured in a successful form of doubling which bolsters the visual impression of disguise. Dissimulation, however, cannot serve the monomaniac: it undoes him as do his disguises. He cannot assume another persona, but is condemned to remain himself in spite of his intentions. The best he can manage is to convert his foibles into consciously entertaining performances. And it is only a privileged class of the monomaniacs in the *Polyandre* which reaches this level and partially succeeds in overcoming some very obvious flaws. Doomed to an almost intrareferential discourse, the monomaniac experiences the same setbacks at the verbal level as he encoun-ters at the physical: his lies are as transparent as his costumes; in attempting to dissimulate, he reveals most unflattering truths.

## Portraiture

The use of the portrait is nearly as ubiquitous as the use of disguise in Sorel's comic novels. Although this item is part of the literary stock of the period, Sorel uses it for his own sarcas-tic ends with an arresting regularity. Portraits punctuate the intrigues of the *Francion* and the *Polyandre*, and the portrait of Charite in the *Berger* assumes the role of a satirical emblem which signifies the novel's intent to ridicule all outrageous simi-les and metaphors. The choice of the portrait for these functions is most felicitous, for, like disguise, it embodies *per se* the di-lemma of illusion and reality and thus inherently sums up the comic novel's principal preoccupation with the distinction between *être* and *paraître*, for the portrait, itself an artifact, may be a mimetic representation of reality or a conscious distor-tion. As in the case of any costume, its representational accuracy must always be verified.

The portrait of Nays in the *Francion* has a very dramatic im-pact on the development of the intrigue. Francion, previously informed of Laurette's infidelity, espies the portrait from his sickbed and immediately waxes ecstatic. Raymond replies to his anxious queries by informing him that it is the portrait of an Italian beauty whose relative will shortly be visiting the castle. The portrait's place in the intrigue emphatically makes it the first sign of Francion's emotional liberation from Laurette, the harlot whom he mistook for an ideal lover. Henceforth, his attention will basically be fixed, in spite of numerous aberrant adventures, on the quest for Nays. But, by the same token and completely in line with the dangers of disguise, the portrait becomes the source of new anguish: is it really a faithful representation of Nays? On one level, a new contest between reality and illusion has been initiated. Francion must confirm the fidelity of the portrait in order to be certain that he is not once more enslaved to a false image. In that sense, the portrait dilemma offers a more concrete demonstration of the fact that he has learned from the Laurette intrigue.

The portrait scene also occurs in the context of a discussion of the relationship between true perception and amorous pleasure. Raymond has already informed Francion that in matters of the bedroom, one need only close his eyes to enjoy fully any partner.[17] Francion has summarily rejected this position. Pursuing the woman of the portrait, conquering this ideal beauty, is thus presented as one of two conflicting theories of erotic satisfaction, one practical and one idealist (with reservations). Again, this idealism emphasizes the preeminence of reality over fantasy, of truth over fiction. Both clothing and portraits must have a firm correspondence with the real if they are to have any value.

But the portrait of Nays is also a satirical tool. Shortly before his first meeting with this Italian beauty, Francion indulges in a poetic lament over the portrait of his intended mistress. The intense emotion which he expresses in this scene is very tongue-in-cheek, precisely because it is likened to similar situations in novels: "On dit que se laissant aller alors aux imaginations Poëtiques, il fit ceste plainte qui a l'air de celles que l'on trouve dans les Romans" (F, 352). This satirical aspect of the portrait of Nays also links it to disguise, for it shares in the ridicule of literary targets in a manner analogous to the shepherd's costume of the mock pastoral: it is an appropriate accoutrement of the traditional love story, but it is used in an entirely sarcastic context.

When Francion does meet Nays, he recognizes the fidelity of the portrait and begins the rites of courtship in earnest. At this point, one aspect of the illusion game is brought to a close: the representational accuracy of the portrait has been confirmed. The same rigorous insistence on truth has been applied to portraiture as to clothing.

The portrait of Charite in the *Berger* appears nearly at the beginning of the work and assumes an emblematic role. Painted by Anselme for Lysis, it adheres literally to the conventions of physical description found in novels and poetry; it becomes a concretization of almost every cliché on feminine beauty, a visual parody. This portrait displays marked affinities with the masquerades of the monomaniacs. The features of their disguises which were intended to increase their stature—swords, boots, braids—all turn against them in humiliating exposures of their true identities. Likewise, the literalized clichés of the portrait of Charite—her lips of coral, the hearts dangling from her locks, the two hemispheres for her breasts—turn the portrait into a kind of monster and render Lysis' admiration thoroughly ludicrous.

The temptation of the portrait proved so strong that Sorel inserted even a second portrait in the *Berger*: that of the "menuisier gentilhomme" in Carmelin's tale. This story is an elaborate play on appearance and reality. A pompous carpenter has himself painted as a nobleman. The artist, who decides to teach him a lesson, tells the carpenter to wipe the portrait when he displays it to his friends. The would-be nobleman follows the instruction, only to discover a new portrait hidden under the surface: that of a "menuisier cornu." This time fiction is brought into line with reality in a disastrous fashion, for illusion disappears to reveal the carpenter's disgrace. The movement is characteristically negative, conferring a consistent tone of sarcasm upon the use of portraiture. It also parallels the monomaniacs' difficulties with disguise in that it once again effects the surprise reversal of situations, moving from the flattering to the humiliating.

The first portrait in the *Polyandre* is more mysterious and polyvalent. It is introduced at the very beginning of the novel, when Musigène, in a seizure of poetic ecstacy, kneels before a crowd of women to adore the portrait of the unknown beauty he beholds. The poet is already a ludicrous sight in his ill-fitting, worn clothing. His gesture instantly becomes another satirical allusion to the role of portraits in novels and, possibly, a veiled reference to the adoration scene of the *Francion*. His effusions are interrupted by the arrival of an unknown gentleman, who brusquely snatches the portrait from him and disappears into the crowd. The bevy of female spectators immediately begins speculating on the identity of the woman in the portrait, and thus another mystery sequence is initiated.

The suspense is broken only much later, when Polyandre tells a convoluted tale of the portrait's passage into various hands. The original owner and subject of the portrait, Céphize, had gone through an intricate series of efforts to regain it. Due to a tumultuous love life, she concludes the intrigue by fleeing to a convent, to everyone's disappointment. But Polyandre uses this tale to his own ends. He tells Néophile that Céphize has really locked herself up in a convent because she has despaired of the young man's affections. This is a complete fabrication. As the text puts it: "Polyandre disoit ces choses pour flatter Néophile, et contenter la vanité d'une personne qui cherchoit de tous costez de quoy se satisfaire. La plus grande partie de ce qu'il disoit estoit inventé à plaisir selon l'occasion" (P, I, 285). Thus, in the hands of the hero, the portrait functions very much like a disguise: a fiction in itself, it engenders a new series of fictions used to feed Néophile's sense of self-importance. It becomes another means of exploiting the gullible.

But the mysterious portrait is not abandoned here. Later on, the coquette Clorinie will also refer to the portrait. Appropriately, she imagines that it is her own. Convinced of her irresistibility (though she has no appeal for Polyandre), she comments upon it and thus, by becoming her own dupe, illustrates the fatal role of vanity in all of Sorel's novels. Her reaction seems analogous to Hortensius' behavior in the King of Poland episode. Supplied with appropriate regalia, the pedant believes himself a king. Here the simple existence of a portrait substitutes for items of costume and serves as the pretext for unwarranted fantasy.

To complicate matters further and to expand the theme of vanity, Clorinie also owns a portrait of herself which she has changed daily: the artist comes to readjust her *mouches*. Here, taken to the extreme, the portrait is transformed into a joke: forced to a degree of representational fidelity which far exceeds reason, the whole purpose of portraits is put into question. In a sense, this *reductio ad absurdam* is related to the portrait of Charite, because representational accuracy is exaggerated to the point of the ridiculous in a manner similar to the literal reading of metaphors in depicting Lysis' ideal woman. The portrait becomes, like clothing, a misunderstood symbol to the ignorant who are trapped in exteriors. Clorinie has taken things too far and failed to grasp the purpose of portraiture.

Clearly, Sorel was extremely attracted to the use of portraits in the comic novel. In fact, he found this theme so alluring that he even devoted an entire tale to the subject: "Description de l'isle de portraiture et de la ville des portraits,"[18] a work which explores some of the most fantastic possibilities of portrait painting and links it to disguise. In this story, the whole island is inhabited by people who play at illusion, who wear masks that are so natural as to appear as their real faces. This preference for masquerade is complimented by the island's painters, who, with a taste for the grotesque, apply the principles of the *Berger*, which is mentioned in the text, by their literal depiction of literary clichés. Portraiture and disguise become synonymous with writing, an allegory of the narrative process. Indeed, the tale to some extent justifies the comic novel, for one visitor to the island chooses to apprentice himself to the comic rather than to the satiric painters because of a certain lack of discernment in the latter: their vision is too grim. Though Sorel does not always distinguish very well between the comic and the satirical genres,[19] it is evident here that he sees the comic novel as a combination of *l'agréable et l'utile* more effective than the satirical, in that humor is a more appealing and more persuasive stratagem than sour mockery. Surely, the numerous portraits and disguises of the comic novels realize Sorel's objectives: they entertain, but simultaneously admonish. To that degree, they are consistent with the didactic intent of those novels.

Since the portrait as a stock device so admirably suits the needs and objectives of Sorel's comic novels, it is hardly surprising that it plays such a major role in his works. The very emblem of the struggle between illusion and reality, it is natural that the portrait should function as an analogue of disguise. It is a most polyvalent device and, like disguise, plays both serious and comic roles. A symbol of the world of appearances, it initiates games and creates ever more involved webs of illusion. In the labyrinthine intrigues of Sorel's comic novels, it serves as a *point de repère*, ever insisting on the basic theme and creating, if nothing else, an ideological unity for Sorel's work.

Thus, portraiture and language reinforce the patterns which characterize disguise, and, in doing so, they demonstrate the overall coherence of Sorel's works. They are different "codes" which send similar messages: like disguise, they share in satirizing contemporary literature and they develop the complex contests of the illusion game. They function as part of a unified program with definite objectives and a very consistent *modus operandi*. Portraiture and language thereby evidence the extraordinary harmony of Sorel's comic novels.

Disguise itself, closely and cleverly allied to its analogues in language and portraiture, enjoys an ambiguous, multifaceted relationship with *paraître*. It can paradoxically surpass its role of concealment and exalt those who use it, as in the libertine orgy. It may undo the disguised character by betraying his ambitions, reducing him to an object of humiliation, and rendering him the butt of sarcasms, as is universally the case with the monomaniacs. It may also prove an effective aid in furthering the ambitions of the novels' heroes as well as another means of differentiating them from their fellow characters. Disguise is characterized by enormous fluidity and "downward" mobility, but, strangely enough, it never completely undermines reality, which remains stable, unshakable: all things are set aright in the end and no character ever remains permanently outside his caste due to a change of costume. In fact, the assumption that there is something solid beyond appearances underlies all the comic novels.[20] This certainty is allied to Sorel's notion of realism, and his playful abuse of *paraître* is one manner of referring the reader to things as they are, to a certain notion of social truth which itself remains aloof from skepticism. Given this act of faith in a ground of social verity, as opposed to a totally unanchored, protean fluidity, the efficacy of disguise must perforce be limited to specific persons. It is, thus, useless in the hands of the peasant seeking to be upwardly mobile (who, in fact, cannot exist in Sorel's opus) or the poetaster; their very essences deny them mobility.[21]

For the most part, disguise, like its analogue, language, embodies a form of aggression—successful or unsuccessful, depending on the character; it is a playful way of dominating others, of manipulating them for comic designs. Its mastery is rigidly related to class and quality. But its use in Sorel's comic novels far exceeds his need for realism. Rather, it serves as an expression of the cultural ambient which understood the world as a theater of maneuver and surprise. Rich in its skeptical implications, disguise heralds a world in which the belief in essences was to dissolve and class structure was consequently to be undermined. But its expression in Sorel only hints at the corrosive potentials of the play of appearance. It remains for him one of the most tantalizing aspects of the illusion game, one of the most entertaining devices of the comic novel.

# CONCLUSIONS

Starting out with a novel of lucidity which simultaneously attacked literature and the prejudices of society, Sorel seemed off to a prodigious start. The struggles of the young Francion comprise the great libertine novel of apprenticeship, for they combine a demand for immediate sensual gratification with an intense intellectual curiosity. In many ways, these traits are inseparable, for knowledge yields both power and pleasure in the libertine universe. With the *Francion*, Sorel took the tradition of the *picaro* and uplifted it by allying it to the boldest thinking of his time.

But with the *Berger*, Sorel shifted emphasis and undid the hero. In fact, the *Berger* might be termed the *Francion* in reverse. Its gifted but perverse hero Lysis moves in the opposite direction to that of his predecessor, for he seeks not lucidity, but obfuscation in a life that follows fiction rather than reality. And so the dynamic struggle for clear perception and its rigorous application to the world disappears in favor of a *deus ex machina*, Clarimond, who sets the wayward Lysis aright. There can be no empathy with the protagonist, only disapproving distance. More importantly, perhaps, was Sorel's narrowing of critical focus. The *Berger* or the *Anti-roman* became so excessively bent on literary satire that it lost the breadth of social criticism which characterized the *Francion* and deteriorated into an over-extended parody of novelistic abuses. Beating a dead horse is rarely the road to great literature. But then, in all fairness, Sorel was consciously fleeing literature, and his work does clear the way by its very critique for more accurate character portrayal, for more "realism" in the novel. But the *Berger* is too vast a work of destruction; it contains too much satire and too little insight. It is, nevertheless, a feast for the twentieth-century critic, for it exhibits all the narcissism, all the sterile cleverness of the current self-reflexive novels and films.

The *Polyandre* was the logical, if delayed, follow-up to the *Berger* because, once Sorel had laid bare the flaws of the contemporary novel, he needed to try to develop a work more in keeping with what "realistic" literature could be: a comedy of manners, a close-up study of types drawn from daily existence. Rejecting the contemporary novel, Sorel sought a new verisimilitude, a new truth akin to that which he envisioned for the *nouvelle* in his meticulous, if not laborious, portrayal of the Parisian scene. But the *Polyandre* failed. Its hero has no secret qualities or hidden philosophy. Blandly perfect and devoid of any passion for truth, he is merely adept at social advancement. No inner fire of youthful indignation puts him at odds with the world. His very self-assurance—the very smugness implicit in the novel's author—immediately deprives him of any interest. Francion's qualities have deteriorated into mere deviousness. Sorel's satire of literature, while ever-present, has also lost its edge—in part because it is subservient to a not particularly lively form of social satire. One feels that the *Polyandre* is almost a formula novel: the appropriate collection of types is mechanically joined together to give an impression of everyday life among the *noblesse de robe*, the newly emergent *haute bourgeoisie*.

From the perspective of the illusion game, these novels follow a descending trajectory: at its most piquant in the *Francion*, the illusion game becomes pedantic in the *Berger* and facile in the *Polyandre*, indeed, too predictable, almost lazy. My judgment must agree with traditional evaluations of Sorel's comic novels. He emerges full of promise, only to become the victim of his own verbose indignation. He did turn to "higher" endeavors, but proved incapable of the greatness they required. As an historiographer, he produced no more than panegyrics of the French monarchy;[1] as a philosopher, in his *La Science universelle*, he compiled not a summa, but a rambling catalogue of all human knowledge, an unsuccessful encyclopedia. Sorel was a man whose intellectual ambitions greatly exceeded his talents. The nasty, carping, hypercritical Charroselles of Furetière was to some degree a caricature Sorel had brought upon himself. A negativity unredeemed by sufficient creativity must be seen as one of his most damaging traits.

But it would be unfair and unduly cruel—too Sorelian—to part on such a sour note. The *Francion* and, to some extent, the *Berger* assure Sorel a place of permanent importance in French literary history. The first is not only a solid novel of apprenticeship, but an unquestionably outstanding work as well, the apotheosis of the libertine credo. Furthermore, both the *Francion* and, more emphatically, the *Berger* or *Anti-roman* qualify Sorel as one of the great deconstructors of the novel. He blazed a path which eventually led to a re-examination of the genre. His kinship with Scarron, Furetière, and Diderot in the following century is clear. Further, as one who demanded an end to the innumerable travesties, to the unnaturally long courtships, and the wretchedly escapist tales of shepherds and knights, he deserves recognition and gratitude. As a writer who dared to speak out for the demands of sexual gratification and who recognized the importance of financial concerns, as a writer who, in short, demanded that literature approach life and that the escapist ideals of his time be discarded in favor of the elements of daily existence, Sorel asserted himself as a key figure in the ideological critique of the seventeenth-century novel. This obtains equally well in stylistics, where his sarcastic parodies of florid speech and his manipulation of the *galimatias* show that he was just as concerned with the use of language as he was with the subjects it treated. He stands as a major contributor to the dialectic between the novel and the anti-novel. Craftily, he opened a debate which not only criticized the novel from without, but also interiorized itself within that very genre and undermined the conventions that governed it. The comic novels, most especially the first two, are Sorel's internal subversion. At the same time, almost despite himself, he continued to write literature, applying with mixed success the principles he espoused. And so he escapes the condemnation of being totally negative, for he was more than willing to consecrate the necessary effort for the reform or replacement of the contemporary novel with fictional works more suitable to his times, namely, the *Polyandre* and the *Nouvelles*. Acutely sensitive to the "lies" of novels, he used the conflict between *être* and *paraître* as a framework for exposing their absurdity and producing a new literature. Sorel, the master of illusion, made it serve his own special, paradoxical end: the revelation of the truth.

*Appendix A* [1]


*HISTOIRE COMIQUE DE FRANCION*
(Adam Edition with Its Book Order)


*Book I*
Night adventures:
- —Valentin's bath and capture.
- —Laurette receives Olivier in place of Francion.
- —Francion is shaken off his ladder while scaling the castle wall and lands in Valentin's tun.
- —Laurette and Olivier subdue Catherine and suspend her from the castle wall with his/her "secrettes parties" revealed.

Morning:
- —Catherine is discovered by the villagers.
- —Valentin is discovered by the local curé and peasants.

Francion:
- —The injured hero jokes with the surgeon at the inn.
- —He escapes from the inn in a cart.
- —He arrives at another village at night and lodges in a tavern where he meets a nobleman and begins the story of his passion for Laurette.


*Book II*
While dreaming, Francion nearly makes love to the aged procuress, Agathe.
- —Awakened by the nobleman's laughter, Francion flies into a rage.

Agathe's stories:
- —Agathe's career as a prostitute and then as a procuress.
- —Career of Laurette, Agathe's adopted child and accomplished prostitute.

Francion reasserts his belief in Laurette's affection for him despite Agathe's tale.

*Book III*
Francion is invited to the nobleman's castle.
Francion recounts his dream, which begins and ends with frustration:
  —An ever-receding island and inaccessible mistress encased in glass.
Arrival at castle:
  —Story of Francion's father's problems with lawyers.
  —Story of the child Francion; his victories over superstitious and dishonest servants.
  —Story of the miseries of "collège" under the tutelage of Hortensius.
Francion becomes entranced with the portrait of Nays.

*Book IV*
More tales of "collège":
  —Idiocy of the curriculum.
  —Vengeance against Hortensius on the stage.
  —Hortensius' courtship of Frémonde.
Francion's "dépucelage": he mistakes a hag for a beautiful servant.
Post-educational poverty:
  —Clothing episodes.
  —Francion decides to study poetry.
Story of Raymond's theft and the nobleman's promise to look into it.

*Book V*
Francion continues to study poetry and makes the acquaintance of poets.
Francion's mother sends him money and ends his poverty:
  —Courtship of Diane.
  —"La bande des généreux," which, under Francion's direction, humiliates the pretentious.
Francion and Clérante:
  —Francion meets Clérante through Luce.
  —Francion defends Clérante against a satire written about him.
  —Francion is invited to live at Clérante's residence.
  —Arrival of Collinet, the madman, at Clérante's.
  —Beginning of courtship of Luce.

*Book VI*
Courtship of Luce:
  —Francion writes a love letter for Clérante.
  —Francion seduces both Luce and Fleurance.

Clérante and Francion withdraw to the country.

Peasant marriage:

–Francion and Clérante attend disguised as itinerant musicians.

–Francion puts a laxative in the food, and he and Clérante observe the results.

–The disguised Clérante makes overtures to a witty and beautiful "Bourgeoise," whose favors he enjoys.

Sequel to the "Bourgeoise" intrigue:

–Clérante visits her without disguise and vanquishes her through his knowledge of her previous misconduct.

Clérante and Francion return to court.

Count Bajamond story:

–Francion offends the count.

–The count has him ambushed, but Francion escapes.

–Francion defeats Bajamond in a duel, but spares his life.

–Francion continues to enjoy the King's good graces.

Francion's noble host announces that he is Raymond and threatens Francion with a fate which he will learn on the following day.

*Book VII*

Libertine orgy:

–Francion, richly dressed, discovers that he is not a victim, but an honored guest.

–Collinet greets him.

–Francion is "condemned" to Laurette.

–He jokes about Agathe.

–Francion proclaims his theory of free love.

–He inquires about Nays.

Valentin arrives at the castle, but is told Laurette is not there.

Quest for Nays:

–Francion reunites a quarreling innkeeper and his wife.

–Francion learns of the miser Du Buisson's greed.

*Book IX*

Miser episode:

–Francion reforms Du Buisson and arranges for his daughter's marriage.

Nays:

–Prelude to meeting: adoration of her portrait.

–Francion tries to pass for Floriandre, her dead lover.

–Francion, after having established his real identity, courts Nays in earnest.

–Francion plays a joke on his rivals, Ergaste and Valère.

—They lure him into trying a "magic" chair which dumps him into a trench, and they inform Nays that he has gone back to France, sending her a forged letter of rejection.

Anti-pastoral:

—Francion, delivered from his prison by the kindness of his jailer, becomes a shepherd.

—Francion plays the lute, seduces young peasants, and gains a reputation as a magician.

## Book X

Joconde:

—Still dressed as a peasant, Francion seduces Joconde.

—He is injured fleeing Joconde's quarters.

"Le Vieillard goutteux":

—The wounded Francion places himself in the "chaire a bras" of the old conspirator who has just left.

—He is carried before the Governor of the city, but is released when the error is discovered.

Return to France and resumption of quest:

—Francion exchanges costumes with a soldier.

—He plays the charlatan and dupes a village of peasants.

—After reaching Lyons and re-equipping himself, Francion returns to Rome and is reunited with Nays.

News of Hortensius:

—Various tales of Hortensius' discomfiture in Paris, most notably the Saluste and boots stories.

## Book XI

Return of Hortensius:

—Hortensius announces his various literary projects; his compliments to Francion prove to be plagiarized.

—Francion reveals his own literary achievements and theories to Raymond and compares them with those of Hortensius.

Marriage of Francion and Nays.

## Book XII

Francion's marriage in jeopardy:

—He is accused of writing a marriage promise to Emilie (plot of Ergaste).

—He is also arrested for counterfeiting (plot of Valère).

—Nays is disenchanted by his infidelity.

—Public trial exonerates Francion of all charges.

—Ergaste is condemned to marry Emilie; Valère is exiled.

—A somewhat difficult Nays consents to marriage with Francion.

*Appendix B*


## *LE BERGER EXTRAVAGANT*
## (1627 Edition, Slatkine Rpt.)


*Book I*

Lysis (Louis), a young bourgeois who has fled Paris for St. Cloud to live the pastoral, addresses his mangy flock.

He meets Anselme and tells him of his meeting with Charite (Catherine), a serving girl, with whom he is passionately in love.

Adrian, Lysis' relative and warden, arrives and attempts to take him back to Paris.

Lysis communicates Charite's beauties and his sufferings to a shepherd, using metaphor; the shepherd takes him literally.

Lysis consults Echo and debates Anselme on the validity of the Echo myth.

Lysis commissions Anselme to make a portrait of Charite.

Lysis' description of Charite to the shepherd is transformed into news of the coming of the Anti-Christ. A panic ensues among the local peasantry.

Adrian has Lysis' flock butchered; the latter is furious.

Lysis, who wishes to go to Forez, is placed in the care of Anselme by an overly trusting Adrian. Anselme plans to enjoy Lysis's folly.

*Book II*

Lysis does not find Anselme's library to his liking; it is too philosophical.

Lysis attacks the "satyr" (a peasant) who has kissed Charite.

Anselme gives Lysis the portrait of Charite; after a suitable explanation, Lysis becomes enraptured with it.

Anselme recounts the Genèvre story. Lysis, acting as judge, absolves him from any further responsibility to that woman.

Lysis serenades his mistress: a disaster.

Lysis writes Charite a love letter, but is seized as a robber when he attempts to deliver it.

Léonore shows Lysis' letter to Anselme.

Lysis exasperates Charite with his attentions.

Gringalet, a lackey, sets Lysis' hat on fire with a burning mirror; Lysis attributes the conflagration to Charite's gaze.

Anselme explains to Lysis how he has caught the nymph Echo and placed her in a box.

Anselme and Lysis return to Paris to find Léonore, Angélique, and Charite. Anselme plans a departure for Brie, pretending to Lysis that they are going to Forez.

*Book III*

Lysis accompanies Anselme to the Hôtel de Bourgogne, and, taking a pastoral play for reality, he intervenes in the spectacle, to the discomfiture of the actors and the spectators.

Montenor reads Clarimond's *Le Banquet des Dieux*, which Clarimond later explains as his reaction to the absurdities of legends.

Upon his arrival in Forez (Brie), Lysis kisses the ground in reverence.

Lysis meets Clarimond and discusses the *Banquet.*

*Book IV*

At Montenor's, Lysis eats only seven morsels of everything served in honor of the seven letters in Charite's name.

Clarimond promises to put Lysis' story in prose. Two poems are presented: Clarimond's "Adieu à la poésie" and Lysis's "Plainte de Lysis."

Lysis, distracted during another serenade, gets lost in the woods and, after sleeping there, sets out on a new adventure.

Lysis meets a hermit, who misunderstands his praise of Charite for talk about divine love.

Lysis next meets Hircan, whom he takes for a magician; the latter transforms him into "Amarylle," a serving girl, so that he can work in Léonore's household near his beloved Charite.

"Amarylle" is accused of "impudicité" and, despite her success at the ordeal of "la platine sacrée," is condemned to be burned alive as a sorceress. She is delivered from her fate by Hircan at the very last moment.

Lysis, restored to his manly guise, frightens Charite with his poetic discourse.

Lysis meets some peasants who insist they are in Brie, not Forez, and learns that he has been deceived.

Lysis meets Carmelin and takes him into his service.

Lysis proposes to Charite "que nous facions ensemble l'Androgine" and causes her to flee.

Lysis visits Hircan's garden and has an argument with Fontenay, who accuses him of being the successor of Don Quixote.

Lysis writes a *poulet* to Charite, and Carmelin is charged with delivering it.

Lysis and his dog Musidore are seized by peasants for eating grapes that do not belong to him. He is liberated by Hircan, the local lord.

Synope, pretending she is Charite, takes the *poulet* from Carmelin and charges him to tell his master that her anger will never end. Lysis, deeply depressed, decides to spend the night out of doors.

*Book V*

Lysis announces that he is going to be metamorphosed. He becomes a tree: a weeping willow. Despite the pleadings of his friends, he refuses to leave his perch.

That night, Lysis is visited by three "nymphs" and he meets the "Dieu de la Rivière de Morin" and other deities—his friends in various disguises. The nymphs Synope and Lucide recount their stories after Synope has told the tale of Morin.

The following day, Lysis, the willow, narrates his adventures to Carmelin, who keeps watch that night to see the nymphs. A new series of night-time adventures occurs. Carmelin is whipped, and Lysis returns from a banquet with the aquatic deities to find that his tree has been removed. Hircan uses his magic powers to restore the recalcitrant Lysis to humanity.

*Book VI*

As a result of a discussion between Lysis and his friends, a call is sent out to all the poets in Paris to come to Brie and join Lysis in his pastoral republic.

Charite commands Lysis not to obey her any more.

Anselme gives Lysis the box with the "Echo of St. Cloud" in it.

Lysis learns of Charite's illness from an apothecary and demands the same purges as his mistress. He imitates all the aspects of her illness.

Lysis fails miserably as a shepherd: he causes his flock to make a "roüe perpetuelle" around a tree.

Philiris, the first of Lysis' disciples, arrives.

Polidor and Méliante, two "Persians," appear on the scene.

*Book VII*

The narrator comments on suspense techniques and explains the identities of Philiris, Polydor, and Méliante.

Fontenay recounts his tale of narcissism, and then Philiris tells his own story. Lysis is upset because they are both married, a contravention of the pastoral.

### Book VIII

Polidor and Méliante recount their exotic Persian adventure stories. Carmelin then tells his own story, a farce, which Clarimond prefers to the others.

A discussion begins with Clarimond about how to begin Lysis' story.

Lysis finds the wigs of the aquatic masquerade in Hircan's cabinet, but the latter tells him a story of how he rendered those divinities bald.

Hircan prophesizes that Lysis will deliver Panphilie, Méliante's mistress, from captivity.

### Book IX

Oronte gives a feast.

Two "Pasteurs Parisiens" arrive to seek out Lysis. They inform a disdainful Clarimond that many people do not like his *Banquet des Dieux*.

Lysis and company go to a peasant marriage and annoy the peasants, who feel they are being mocked.

Clarimond is sarcastic about the golden age Lysis believes himself to be heralding. The former proposes that they put on plays in which each actor chooses a set linguistic style (metaphors, equivocations, etc.). The plays are to be grotesques.

Lysis goes to bathe in the Morin in the vain hope of re-encountering its aquatic deities. His adventures end with him falling into a trench.

The first play, *Le Ravissement de Proserpine*, is performed. Adrian arrives during the performance and is somewhat shocked by Lysis' behavior, which Anselme explains as part of his acting. Temporarily soothed, Adrian states that he will pick up Lysis on the way back from his pilgrimage.

The next day, *La Toison d'or* is performed.

Hircan promises to make Lysis and Carmelin invulnerable for their mission to deliver Méliante's mistress.

### Book X

Lysis and Carmelin, dressed for the occasion, go on an heroic mission in a coach drawn by flying horses to deliver "Panphilie." They do so after a combat with "giants" and a "dragon."

Upon his return, Lysis recounts his fantastic and untruthful adventures.

Lysis goes hunting dressed as an antique hero.

Hircan tells the story of the magician Anaximandre, Panphilie's captor.

Lysis decides that the more compliant Philiris will be his historiographer, rather than the difficult Clarimond. There is a discussion of Lysis' novel.

## Book XI

Anselme, to justify himself to Angélique, recounts the story of Clarice. He is supported by Montenor, who tells the story of Alican.

Carmelin, at the behest of Amarylle, recounts his own version of the deliverance of "Panphilie."

A triumph of Bacchus is celebrated.

Night adventure: Lysis tries to carry off Charite, who is, in fact, no more than a log dressed in articles of her clothing. He inadvertently interrupts a tryst between Anselme and Angélique.

Betrothal of Anselme and Angélique.

Wedding of Hircan and Amarylle.

Adrian arrives, but is held in check by Hircan's "magic." The latter makes Adrian believe that he has been rendered deaf.

During all this, Anselme and Angélique are married.

Fontenay tells a doubting Adrian the story of Lysis' adventures.

## Book XII

Adrian, in the company of other "shepherds," seeks out Lysis at his hideaway.

Lysis discovers that his flock has been sold for slaughter to pay his rent.

Adrian is confused by the universal confirmation of Lysis' adventures.

Clarimond agrees to help Adrian in saving Lysis from his follies.

Lysis plans and carries out a faked suicide; he is "resuscitated" by the eyes of Charite.

Musardan, the author, visits Hircan.

A debate is proposed between Clarimond and Musardan on the utility of novels and poetry.

## Book XIII

Clarimond begins his attack on literature with Homer and eventually reaches the *Astrée*.

Musardan is incapable of countering Clarimond's arguments and is booed.

Philiris takes up the defense.

Amarylle intervenes in favor of novels.

Anselme gives a favorable, but reserved, judgment: novels are written for pleasure, not for instruction.

*Book XIV*

At Clarimond's instigation, the assembly decides that it is time for Lysis' cure.

Just as during their previous meeting, the hermit preaches to Lysis and initially misunderstands him.

Clarimond makes a detailed refutation of all Lysis' follies and justifies all the trickery as merited by Lysis' self-deception.

Lysis is persuaded to abandon his shepherd's ways and is married to Charite.

Carmelin weds Lisette.

Lysis stays in Brie under the surveillance of Clarimond and leads the life of a "gentil-homme champestre."

The narrator concludes by casting doubts on the authenticity of his own story: "une fable pour une histoire."

*Appendix C*


*POLYANDRE: HISTOIRE COMIQUE*
(1648 Edition, Slatkine Rpt.)


Part I

*Book I*
Polyandre, who has just returned to Paris, notices Musigène, the *poète crotté*, who is adoring a portrait before a crowd of women.
The portrait is suddenly seized by an unknown man.
Polyandre meets Musigène and then Néophile.
Néophile visits Aurélie, but mistakenly offers his homage to her maid, an old hag called Guérinette. Believing that a trick has been played on him, he storms out of Aurélie's residence, refusing even to hear her explanation of what has occurred.
Néophile and two gentlemen meet Polyandre and Musigène as Néophile departs from Aurélie's. They all enter his carriage; he complains and the others offer him advice:
—Musigène maintains that the key to success in love is to write good verse.
—Orilan preaches multiple devotion rather than absolute fidelity.
—A venerable old man (later revealed as the charlatan, Héliodore-Théophraste) tells Néophile that he must go to extraordinary expense if he wishes to be successful in love. He lures Néophile out of the carriage, tells him about the philosopher's stone, and wangles a sum of money from him.
As the traffic jam clears and the company travels on, Orilan continues with his antics as a universal lover. The carriage arrives at Néophile's court-

yard. Orilan is stopped by some household clerks who enjoy his stories. Polyandre and Néophile are glad to be rid of him.

## Book II

Polyandre explains to Néophile that the incident at Aurélie's was an accident; he also comments on the eccentricity of characters like Musigène and Orilan and identifies the old man as an alchemist.

After dinner at Aesculan's (Néophile's father), Néophile, Polyandre, and company go to a ball given by a financier. It is interrupted by some noble party crashers, one of whom is killed in a duel. Orilan has his wig lifted by Polyandre.

The story of Céphize is told by a guest in Aesculan's household and continued by Polyandre, who invents part of the story to flatter Néophile.

Musigène and Gastrimargue argue over the worth of the former's poem. When Gastrimargue leaves the dinner, the irritated Musigène tells the story of Gastrimargue from his conception to his present situation as glutton, parasite, and miser.

Musigène receives a gift of money from Aesculan for his tale and contemplates buying some badly needed new clothes.

## Book III

Musigène is arrested for wearing a gold braid or trim (*cordon*) in violation of the king's edict. He reveals that it is actually straw. Polyandre delivers Musigène from his captors by a ruse.

Musigène and Polyandre visit Aurélie to reconcile her and Néophile. Aurélie explains her maid's curious behavior.

Polyandre persuades Néophile to apologize, but when they go to Aurélie's, she is not at home. They decide to go to the Foire St.-Germain. In the bustle of the fair, they encounter Orilan, who arrives surrounded by lackeys and preceded by a page crying "Place, voicy le Roy des Amoureux." Polyandre delivers him from this mob. Freed, Orilan engages in more zany "galanteries," to the exasperation of several lady shopkeepers.

Polyandre's friend, Cléobule, recounts the various love escapades of Néophile, which include disguise episodes and the entanglements of a marriage promise.

## Part II

## Book IV

The book opens with a visit to the home of Clorinie, an "Archi-coquette." There is a discussion of the portrait of Céphize, which Clorinie thinks is her own.

Mélinte recounts the story of Héliodore and Artéphius, two charlatans posing as masters of alchemy. Mélinte concludes his story with the news that Héliodore is now in Paris going by the name Théophraste. Clorinie is disconcerted, since she is one of his victims.

Mélinte continues the story of Héliodore-Théophraste with the latter's attempt to dupe Péralde and Philomire. The tale ends with an argument between Mélinte and Clorinie, who insists that there must be two Théophrastes in Paris rather than admitting she has been tricked.

*Book V*
Polyandre has fallen in love with Aurélie and goes to visit her. Néophile apologizes to her for his behavior during the Guérinette incident.

Aesculan tells Polyandre that he does not think Néophile is right for Aurélie; he wishes to marry her instead. Polyandre, momentarily taken aback, decides to triumph over both father and son.

During another visit to Aurélie's, Musigène and Orilan also drop by and engage in a comical argument, during which Orilan asserts his superiority over Hylas in the *Astrée*. Mme Ragonde, the ultra-pious relative of Aurélie and Hypéride, arrives—to the confusion and terror of the household. Polyandre disguises himself as "Frère Polycarpe" and delights the old woman with his feigned piety. After she leaves, Polyandre tells the story of Gastrimargue's carriage.

Later on, Polyandre and Néophile go riding in a carriage and leave Musigène to observe Gastrimargue's agony of hunger as a result of a practical joke on the parasite to have the dinner he expected at Aesculan's delayed as long as possible.

Polyandre tells Aesculan, Néophile, and Musigène the story of Gastrimargue's loves.

The news comes that Gastrimargue has been enriched by gifts from a wealthy patron. Musigène is depressed, but is consoled by the promise of a future gift from Aesculan.

# NOTES

## Introduction

1. Charles Sorel, *Histoire comique de Francion*, in *Romanciers du XVII<sup>e</sup> siècle*, ed. Antoine Adam, Bibliothèque de la Pléiade (Paris: Gallimard, 1958). All quotes will be from this edition. The novel will be referred to as the *Francion* throughout this study. It is important to point out that the *Francion*, first published in incomplete form in 1623, was finished in the 1626 edition and then expanded in the 1633 edition. Its expansion had considerable impact on its structural development, as will be indicated in ch. 1. At this point, it would be futile to rehash the debate over Sorel's authorship of the *Francion*—a point which has been generally conceded. The stylistic, thematic, and ideological affinities among the *Francion*, the *Berger*, and the *Polyandre* are so striking that it would be difficult to doubt Sorel's authorship of the first, even without knowing that his contemporaries attributed the novel to him.

2. This study will focus on Charles Sorel's *Le Berger extravagant* (Paris: Toussainct du Bray, 1627; rpt. Geneva: Slatkine, 1972). The main purpose of this restriction is to examine *Le Berger extravagant* as a comic novel like the *Francion* or the *Polyandre*, rather than as a mixed genre composed of a story and critical commentary. The latter situation occurred when Sorel, in the 1628 edition of the *Berger extravagant*, appended a series of "Remarques" on the novel, which in the 1633 edition he moved from the end of the work to the end of the various chapters to which the remarks refer. He entitled this new arrangement *L'Anti-roman ou l'histoire du berger Lysis*. The term *Anti-roman* is used in the text whenever it is necessary to distinguish between the fourteen books of Lysis' adventures and the greater, more complex unity created by those books and the appended remarks. For practical purposes, the 1627 Toussainct du Bray edition will be referred to as simply the *Berger*.

3. Charles Sorel, *Polyandre, histoire comique* (Paris: chez la vefve Nicolas Cercy, 1648; rpt. Geneva: Slatkine, 1972-1974), 2 vols. This work will be referred to as the *Polyandre*.

4. Charles Sorel, *La Bibliothèque françoise* (Paris: La Compagnie des Libraires du Palais, 1667; rpt. Geneva: Slatkine, 1970). All future references will be indicated in the text by the abbreviation BF. Sorel also classified *La Maison des jeux* as a comic novel, but it has not been included in this work for two reasons: first, its format differs significantly from the other comic novels; second, Sorel does not discuss it consecutively, as he does with the other three comic novels in *La Bibliothèque françoise*, and thus sets it apart. In choosing not to treat *La Maison des jeux*, I do not wish to imply

that this novel is unworthy of critical commentary. In fact, it deserves a separate study.

5. Charles Sorel, *De la connoissance des bons livres* (Paris: André Pralard, 1671), p. 102. All future references will be indicated in the text with the abbreviation CBL.

6. Although I first used the term "illusion game" in my thesis, "Illusion and Reality in Sorel's *Francion*" (University of Pennsylvania, 1973), I find it encouraging that another scholar has been intrigued by this aspect of play in Sorel's writing, namely, Susan N. Mayfield, who has made a study of Sorel's novels in her dissertation, "The House of Games: The Fictional Works of Charles Sorel" (The Johns Hopkins University, 1975).

7. La Bruyère, for example, tends to view "honnêteté" as a pose devoid of moral content: "La distance qu'il y a de l'honnête homme à l'habile homme s'affaiblit de jour à autre, et est sur le point de disparaître"; and "On connaît assez qu'un homme de bien est honnête homme; mais il est plaisant d'imaginer que tout honnête homme n'est pas homme de bien." "Des jugements," *Les Caractères* (Paris: Gallimard, 1975), no. 55. As the first reflection indicates, La Bruyère assumes that things have reached a state of decadence. He might well have accepted the existence of true "honnêteté" earlier in the century when Sorel wrote his comic novels.

8. Charles Sorel, *La Maison des jeux* (Paris: Nicolas de Cercy, 1642).

9. In short, he is the first of the great deconstructors of the novel.

10. For an extended discussion of the opening of the *Francion*, see Félix Freudmann, "La Recherche passionnée du *Francion*," *Symposium*, 21 (1967), 103-04.

11. For a discussion of one of the many structural functions of the dream, see A. Suozzo, "Nays as the Vicarious Heroine: The *Francion*'s Book XII," *French Forum*, 3 (1978), 4.

12. For example, Guez de Balzac, Racan, and the pastoral novel.

13. For a particularly subtle discussion of Sorel's use of the word "histoire" and its relationship to "roman" and "nouvelle," see Gabrielle Verdier, "The Art of the *Nouvelle* in Early Seventeenth-Century France: Charles Sorel" (diss. Yale University, 1976), pp. 13-24.

14. A book like *L'Orphize de Chrysante* (Paris: Toussainct du Bray, 1626), which appears to be one of Sorel's "stock" novels, actually contains surprising implicit and explicit sarcastic commentary on then-current literary conventions (see Gabrielle Verdier, "Tradition and 'Textuality' in a Baroque Romance: Charles Sorel's *L'Orphize de Chrysante*," *Kentucky Romance Quarterly*, 26 [1979], 491-508). As more work is done on all Sorel's novels, it may prove that there is less contradiction than one would first think between his program and his novels.

## Chapter I

1. Henri Coulet, *Le Roman jusqu'à la Révolution* (Paris: Armand Colin, 1967), p. 197.

2. F.R. Freudmann, "La Recherche passionnée du *Francion*."

3. W. Leiner, "Le Rêve de Francion: Considérations sur la cohésion intérieure de *L'Histoire comique*," in *La Cohérence intérieure* (Paris: Jean-Michel Place, 1977), pp. 157-75.

4. J. Serroy, "D'un roman à métamorphoses: La composition du *Francion* de Sorel," *Baroque*, 6 (1973), 97-103.

5. A. Suozzo, "Nays as the Vicarious Heroine."

6. F. Garavini, "*Francion* rivisitato: Diacronia d'una struttura," *Saggi e Ricerche di Letteratura Francese*, 14 (1975), 37-107.

7. J. Alter, "C'est moi qui parlons: Le jeu des narrateurs dans *Francion*," *French Forum*, 5 (1980), 99-105.

8. E.M. Tilton, "Charles Sorel, Lawyer, and the Case of the *Berger extravagant*," *Papers on French Seventeenth-Century Literature*, 3 (1975), 78.

9. C.S. Greenberg, "Mediation and Madness: Charles Sorel's *Berger extravagant*" (diss. Cornell University, 1977).

10. See D. Chouinard, "Sorel (anti)romancier et le brouillage du discours," *Etudes Françaises*, 14, Nos. 1-2 (April 1978), 65-91. Another critic, Sigrun Thiessen, sees Sorel's combination of the novel and the subsequent remarks as an unsuccessful attempt to create a new genre: "Der Anti-Roman bliebt auch das einzige Werk seiner 'Gattung.' Das Programm des Erneuerung des Romans durch Verbindung mit der Gattung des 'Essais' wurde von Sorels Zeitgenossen nicht aufgegriffen, und auch er selbst hat es nicht wieder realisiert" (*Charles Sorel: Rekonstruktion einer antiklassizistichen Literatur und Studien zum "Anti-Roman*," Münchener Romantische Arbeiten [Munich: Wilhelm Fink, 1977], p. 173).

11. A.L. Franchetti, *Il "Berger extravagant" di Charles Sorel* (Florence: Olschki, 1977). See also Fausta Garavini, "L'Antiromanzo del filosofo stravagante," *Paragone*, 29, No. 349 (June 1978), 3-25.

12. When Lysis explains to Clarimond how his story should begin, he insists on an *in medias res* opening: "Il faut que mon histoire commence par le milieu . . . c'est ainsi que sont les plus celebres Romans. Il faut entrer petit à petit dans le grand cours de l'histoire & n'en descouvrir le secret au lecteur que le plus tard qu'il sera possible" (BE, 330). While this is clearly ironic, it does bear witness to a very definite notion of structural convention, a universally accepted device for plot arrangement.

13. "Mais il faut que l'Arcadie ancienne, & toutes les autres Contrées champestres cedent au Païs des Forests, & en un mot, il faut que toutes les Bergeries soient tenuës pour inferieures à l'Astrée du Marquis d'Urfé, Ouvrage agreable où il y a tant d'Histoires détachées de differentes especes qui viennent à propos au sujet, qu'on peut dire que l'Autheur y a introduit de toutes les manières d'aventure qu'on se pouvoit imaginer, & que c'est un Roman qui contient plusieurs autres Romans . . ." (CBL, 153).

14. I am limiting myself to the bourgeoises and excluding the peasant seduction because this latter adventure presupposes a different approach to courting and because it is really part of another context—the anti-pastoral.

15. I have tried to distill the characteristics that reappear in all these episodes. Other readers or critics may wish to prepare their own lists of the elements of courtship. In the Joconde seduction, Francion does lack the appropriate clothing, but, as I shall discuss later, this omission is a very deliberate in-joke. See ch. 3, p. 83.

16. See ch. 2, p. 54.

17. "Mon ame s'enflammoit au premier objet qui m'apparoissoit, et de cinquante beautez que j'avois le plus souvent dedans ma fantaisie, je ne pouvois pas discerner laquelle m'agreoit le plus; je les poursuivois toutes ensemble . . ." (F, 240); and "Je ne pouvois mettre entierement mon amour en pas une Dame, parce que je n'en trouvois point qui meritast d'estre parfaitement aymée, et si presque toutes celles qui s'offroyent a moy, me charmoient la raison, encore qu'au jugement de tout le monde, elles eussent fort peu de beauté" (F, 268).

18. Even this scene is not without irony, for Francion's sudden effusions over a mere portrait are clearly a parody of a novelistic topos.

19. Besides the Emilie adventure, the story of Francion's *dépucelage* (F, 211-12) is the only other instance of Francion's defeat in a minor love intrigue. In this episode, he enjoys a repulsive hag who was substituted for the voluptuous servant with whom he hoped to lose his virginity. Upon discovering his error, he is outraged, despite the pleasure he took from the experience, because he has been a dupe of appearances. Later on, in his discussions with Count Raymond, he will insist on the importance of attaining nothing less than the ideal in love.

20. Pp. 27-29 are excerpted and adapted from portions of my article "Nays as the Vicarious Heroine."

21. These affairs are only minor in terms of their brevity, not their structural impact.

22. Greenberg, "Mediation and Madness," p. 111.

23. Elizabeth Meier Tilton, "Concept and Technique in the Anti-Novels of Charles Sorel" (diss. Yale University, 1970), p. 222.

24. As Cornelia Thompson Makiya points out, the actual time frame of the novel is seven consecutive days, but time is expanded in the inserted stories. See her "Charles Sorel's *Polyandre, Histoire comique*: Microcosm of the *Noblesse de robe*" (diss. University of Kentucky, 1974), p. 33.

25. The name is spelled with and without the "h" in the text.

26. For an extended discussion of this contrast, see ch. 2, pp. 61-62.

27. "Or pour vous parler de ce dernier livre que je n'ay pas escrit, mais que j'ay seulement en l'imagination pour ce que je portois la houlette lors que j'y ai songé, son titre sera le Berger extravagant" (F, 438); and "Je pense bien, dit Francion, que dans peu de jours je mettray par escrit mon Berger extravagant . . ." (ibid.).

28. He dismisses the glory of authorship quite simply: "Mais au reste quel plaisir aurois je a faire imprimer un livre sous mon nom, veu qu'aujourd'hui il y a tant de sots qui s'en meslent" (F, 436).

29. Claude Cristin sees Hortensius and Francion as extreme projections of Sorel's literary tendencies: "Hortensius et Francion sont également distants et proches de Sorel lui-même: symétriques, en quelque sorte, de leur source commune. Ils représentent deux projections extrêmes du jeune écrivain, l'une 'négative,' et l'ature 'positive'; ou peut-être deux voies entre lesquelles il devra trouver son chemin," in "Personnage méconnu, œuvre méconnue: Hortensius, Francion et Sorel," *Revue des Sciences Humaines*, No. 137 (January-March 1970), 13.

30. Pp. 33-39 are excerpted and adapted from my article "Peasant Marriage and Libertine Orgy: A Note on Baroque Counterpoint in the *Francion*," *French Review*, 50 (1977), 477-79.

31. Ivanna Bugliani ("Francion eroe libertino," *Saggi e Ricerche di Letteratura Francese*, 7 [1966], 9-68) and René Etiemble ("Un Ecrivain généreux: Charles Sorel," in *Hygiène des lettres*, 5 [*"C'est le bouquet"*] [Paris: Gallimard, 1967], pp. 23-35) are among the admirers of the libertine orgy. Félix R. Freudmann ("La Recherche passionnée du *Francion*") is one of the few to see the orgy as degrading.

32. The idea of alterity used above is taken from Gérard Genette, who remarks that the baroque manifests an acute awareness of "otherness" and that the "other" is actually a deformation of the "same" ("L'Univers réversible," in *Figures I* [Paris: Seuil, 1966], p. 20). As regards the term "grotesque," Francis Bar indicates that it was replaced by "burlesque" around 1650 (*Le Genre burlesque en France au XVII$^e$*

*siècle* [Paris: Editions d'Artrey, 1960], p. xii). Although both "grotesque" and "burlesque" apply specifically to a parody of the classics resituated in totally inappropriate social settings, certain scenes and characters of the *Francion* would seem to parody one another with the same juxtaposition of the base and the lofty. There exists an affinity between the "grotesque" in its strictest sense and the comic procedures of the *Francion*.

33. Etiemble cannot resist underlining the shared *préciosité* of Proust and Sorel: Sorel "souhaite que les généreux inventent 'quelques noms mignards'—disons 'faire catleya'—ces mille mots dont les amants de qualité savent renouveler chacune de leurs passions" ("Un Ecrivain généreux," p. 29).

34. As he puts it: "Pardieu le cul n'est rien que les deux extremitez des cuisses conjointes ensemble. Je prends autant de plaisir a le veoir qu'un sein, n'a-t-il pas la mesme forme" (p. 310).

35. The *Francion* manifests a very ambivalent attitude towards human inequality. Its insistence on innate superiority when it matches its gentleman hero against lords of greater station and its smug assumption of peasant inferiority most accurately typify the aspirations of the ascendant bourgeoisie of the early seventeenth century. Such an upward mobility is hardly surprising when one recalls that, until the royal decree of 22 June 1664, entry into the nobility was not severely restricted: many public offices conferred it. See Roland Mousnier, *Problèmes de stratification sociale* (Paris: Presses Universitaires de France, 1965), pp. 30-31.

36. As he phrases it: "Il est vray qu'il y a tant de Lys & de roses sur son teint que l'on ne s'en fournit point autre part pour orner les portiques de tous les Temples; il est certain aussi que son corps est composé de tant de perles, de diamans & de filets d'or qu'il ne tombe rien d'elle qui ne soit capable d'enrichir un avaricieux le plus insatiable du monde" (BE, 305).

37. One character, Nicanore, uses his teeth as bullets (BE, 310), and another, Cyniphe, literally dies of imagination: blindfolded, he is tricked into thinking that his veins have been opened and succumbs to this illusion of death (BE, 311).

38. As Sorel maintains: "Pour suivre donc nostre stile, sçachez que Carmelin raconte sa vie avec des naïvetez dignes de sa personne. . . . Je vous dy encore un coup, que je ne suis pas de ces sots faiseurs de Romans, qui font parler des bergers & d'autres gens de basse condition, avec des discours aussi subtils que pourroit faire un fort bon esprit" ("Remarques," p. 639).

## Chapter II

1. It should be added that much nuance is possible within this framework. There are occasional intermediary characters, like the prostitutes Laurette and Agathe, who do their share of duping without being heroines. Their special status is linked to the ambivalence of Francion's own role early in the novel, i.e., as a far-from-perfect hero.

2. Here I must differ with Jean Serroy, who approaches Francion's marriage to Nays in Book XII as a demonstration of Francion's growth from promiscuity to monogamy, as his acceptance of finality in profusion. See Serroy, "D'un roman à métamorphoses."

3. See my "Disguise and the Rites of Death and Resurrection in Sorel's *Francion*," *French Review*, 53 (1979), 24.

4. Such reflections lead one to doubt any reform of Francion's libertine tendencies from edition to edition (i.e., from the 1623 to the 1626 edition, as is the case here). Despite the various edifying or exculpating passages inserted in the 1633 edition, the message remains the same. In this case, it is a matter of Francion's open acknowledgement of his own debauchery.

5. "Fermez les yeux, Monsieur, quand vou serez contrainct de baiser un visage qui n'a rien d'attrayant, et vos sens ne lairont pas d'estre chastoüillez du plaisir le plus parfait de l'amour, et si vous esteindrez l'ardeur que vous aviez pour vous joindre a un corps en qui vos yeux trouvent des subjets d'une extreme passion" (F, 182).

6. Incidentally, this passage also illustrates Sorel's modernism. For, while he does exploit the positive aspects of classicism during the episode (most notably in costuming: see ch. 3, p. 88), he trumpets the superiority of the new libertinism over classical debauchery.

7. The relationship between Polyandre and Aesculan and Néophile is hard to describe appropriately. They are Polyandre's masters in the sense that he is seeking to serve or assist Aesculan, who is immensely wealthy, and to benefit from his largesse. As part of this service, Polyandre becomes a companion to Aesculan's son, who, because of the privilege conferred by enormous riches, enjoys a position of social superiority. Yet Néophile is simultaneously Polyandre's inferior because the latter is his mentor, a role which Aesculan clearly assigns to Polyandre.

8. Géliaste circulates the rumor that Néophile's father has been ruined and invents a story about the males of Néophile's family sending their wives to the tomb a week after marriage. Néophile disguises himself as a pauper to substantiate the rumor of his father's ruin (P, I, 573-76).

9. There are, of course, other monomaniacs in the *Francion* (lawyers, poets, and a miser), but their appearances are brief and relatively episodic, whereas substantial portions of the *Polyandre* are devoted to Gastrimargue, Musigène, Orilan, and Théophraste.

10. One may speculate that this moderation was in some way tied to Sorel's maturation, but this is impossible to prove.

11. The *Petit Robert* indicates 1825 as the date of the first use of the term *monomanie* and fixes the usage of *monomane* as between 1829 and 1839 ([Paris: S.N.L., 1972], p. 1107).

12. I am not aiming at an exhaustive catalogue of the novel's monomaniacs, but rather at a discussion of the most important and the most typical.

13. His name is an allusion to Quintus Hortensius, Cicero's friendly and famous rival in oratory, who at one point held the office of consul. See P.G. Woodcock, *Concise Dictionary of Ancient History* (New York: Philosophical Library, 1955), p. 185.

14. See ch. 1, n. 29, for the reference to Claude Cristin.

15. For an account of the three elements of courtship, see ch. 1, p. 24.

16. Pp. 62-67 are excerpted and adapted from my article, "Hortensius and Collinet: Gradations and Implications of Madness in the *Francion*," *Romance Notes*, 20 (1979), 81-86.

17. For a discussion of Sorel's pretentions, see Emile Roy, *La Vie et les œuvres de Charles Sorel, sieur de Souvigny (1602-1674)* (Paris: Hachette, 1891), pp. 1-11.

18. "Générosité" is the common attribute of the elite in the *Francion*. For a good notion of its broad meaning, see its various translations in Randle Cotgrave's *A Dictionairie of the French and English Tongues* (London: Adam Islip, 1611; rpt. New York and Amsterdam: Da Capo Press and Theatrum Orbis Terrarum, 1971).

19. A careful reading of the text would suggest an educated gentleman sent to study law, for not only does Collinet know the legal code, but he is also capable of

handling a sword: "Je suis licencié es Loix . . . au reste j'ay du courage, et s'il est besoin de manier une espée, je m'en acquitteray aussi bien, que pas un gentilhomme de vostre suite" (F, 253). This combination of courage and knowledge is not entirely different from Francion himself, a hero of mixed bourgeois and noble traits.

20. Michel Foucault, *Histoire de la folie à l'âge classique* (Paris, 1961), p. 17. For a more contemporary source for Collinet, see F. Garavini, "La Casa dei giochi," *Paragone*, 26, No. 300 (February 1975), 40-41.

21. Lysis must be dealt with under both categories, for his intelligence, however misguided, allies him to the heroes. He is quite articulate and far more consistent in his use of language than the monomaniacs. On the other hand, his nobly turned phrases are ridiculous in context and as ineffectual as any monomanic utterance. Further, his willful pursuit of illusion combined with a culpable madness places him among the monomaniacs. In short, he is one of Sorel's most ambivalent characters.

22. I use the term "madman" with some reservations. Lysis, though he is frequently referred to as "fou," is a more complex character. If there were some noun for an extravagant person—one not wholly sane or completely insane—that term would best describe Lysis' condition, for his follies are at once willful and demented. It is clear that he is not entirely exempt from responsibility for his actions.

23. He accomplishes the latter quite specifically through the mockery of the character Musardan in Book XIII of the *Berger*.

24. As I have indicated in the quote from the *BF*. See Introduction, p. 12.

25. ". . . tousjours j'avois un Roman caché dessus moy, que je lisois en mettant mes autres livres au devant, de peur que le Regent ne l'apperceust" (F, 183).

26. I doubt that this view will be universally accepted, especially given the works consecrated to the *Berger* or *Anti-Roman* by A.L. Franchetti (ch. 1, n. 11), C. Greenberg (ch. 1, n. 9), and Sigrun Thiessen (ch. 1, n. 10). However, I am speaking to the lively unfolding of plot, not the satirical parodies or the elaborate structural format of the *Berger*.

27. Francion follows a similar procedure in the dream, but, unlike Lysis, he is thoroughly aware that he is not recounting reality, and he does not speak from conviction, but rather as an amused storyteller. Part of his narration may also contain an implicit parody of classical astronomy. See Beverly S. Ridgely, "The Cosmic Voyage in Sorel's *Francion*," *Modern Philology*, 65 (1967-1968), 1-8.

28. ". . . mais pource que l'excellence de son naturel estoit de ne point trouver de sujet de fascherie, où les autres se fussent irritez comme d'un grand affront & d'une extréme offence, il n'en fit que rire, & souslevant son manteau au dessus de sa teste, pour la couvrir comme d'un froc, il dit: il faut faire de necessité Vertu. Les Dames voyant combien je souffre de maux pour elle, en seront plus touchées de compassion. Alors plusieurs se dirent l'un à l'autre qu'il n'estoit point trop fou, de chercher si bien ses commoditez" (P, I, 232).

29. Namely, the story of Gastrimargue as a glutton and parasite, which traces him from his birth to his present status (recounted by Musigène), and the stories of his carriage and of his unsuccessful attempts at marriage (both tales recounted by Polyandre).

30. E.M. Tilton sees Gastrimargue's experience as part of the oscillating motion of the plot, which relies on numerous reversals which, in turn, slow down the pace of the intrigue. This interpretation assumes that Gastrimargue's situation would once more be reversed. See Tilton, "Concept and Technique in the Anti-Novels of Charles Sorel," p. 282.

## Chapter III

1. Pp. 76-84 are excerpted and adapted from portions of my article, "Disguise and the Rites of Death and Resurrection."

2. As Sorel explains: "... il ne se faut point imaginer qu'il y ait aucun moyen de parestre veritablement, sans estre logé dans des Palais somptueux, sans estre superbement vestu, & suivi de quantité de valets ..."; and "Quant aux habits, la grande reigle qu'il y a à donner, c'est d'en changer souvent, & de les avoir toujours les plus à la mode qu'il se pourra." Selections from "Les Loix de la galanterie," in *Nouveau Recueil des pièces les plus agréables de ce temps* (Paris: Nicolas de Sercy, 1643), pp. 3-4, 8.

3. The word used in the text is "oublieux," which, since Francion disguises himself "dans la boutique d'un patissier," can only be a variant of "oublayeur," a wafer-maker. See Randle Cotgrave, *A Dictionarie of the French and English Tongues.*

4. Sorel could be more understanding in dealing with the peasantry. See "La Sœur jalouse," in *Les Nouvelles françoises* (Paris: Pierre Billaine, 1623).

5. For an extended discussion of the function of the juxtaposition of death and sensuality, see Ivana Bugliani, "Francion eroe libertino," pp. 42-48.

6. Honoré d'Urfé, *L'Astrée,* ed. Hugues Vaganay, I (Lyons: Pierre Masson, 1925), pp. 15-17.

7. For a dramatic demonstration of just how degrading such an adventure can be for a nobleman, one need only consider the grotesque pairing of Dom Juan and Charlotte (Molière, *Dom Juan,* II, ii).

8. The variations in disguise episodes, like those of the minor love affairs, offer another example of multiplicity *with* diversity.

9. Here is but part of her description: "Son visage estoit si difforme qu'il devoit faire peur aux petits enfants, & que l'on les pouvoit à bon droit menasser de la faire venir à eux, lors qu'ils cryoient, & qu'ils estoient opiniastres. Sa bouche tortuë s'eslevant vers son oreille gauche, la droitte se pouvoit plaindre de ce qu'elle la quittoit ainsi, comme si elle eust creu l'autre plus digne de l'entendre parler; Son nez gros & relevé estoit un crochet où l'on eust peu pendre toutes sortes d'ustencilles de mesnage; Ses yeux rouges & chassieux sembloient estre deux flambeaux, dont la flamme estant esteinte, la mesche demeuroit ardante" (P, II, 317-18).

10. I am referring to the King of Poland episode, in which Francion uses Hortensius to amuse Nays, and to the "Amarylle" episode, when Anselme uses the travestied Lysis to entertain Angélique and Léonore.

11. And a very dangerous one at that, since historically this occurs between two bitter episodes of religious censorship of literature: the trial of Théophile and Molière's battle with the Congrégation over *Tartuffe.*

12. Lysis is so fancily dressed "qu'avec tout cét équipage il estoit fait à peu pres comme Belleroze, lors qu'il va representer Myrtil à la pastoralle du Berger fidelle" (BE, 19).

13. A.L. Franchetti sees this impossibility of recapturing the past as a double fiction: "Ma se Sorel sembra generalmente sposare il punto di vista di Lysis per il quale la realtà dell' abito coincide con quella dell'essere, non manca poi, al momento giusto, di capovolgere il senso delle sue affermazioni ponendo l'accento sull'impossibilità di riprodurre l'esattezza storica dei costumi: l'abito è dunque finzione duplice, non solo nasconde il vero essere, ma è anche falsa immagine di quella realtà che dovrebbe rappresentare" (*Il "Berger extravagant" di Charles Sorel,* p. 104).

14. Attributed to Sorel, though its author is listed as "le Chevalier de Rozandre" (Paris: Robert Daufresne, 1622).

15. Ibid., p. 4.

16. Ibid., pp. 11-12.

17. See ch. 2, n. 5.

18. Sorel, "Description de l'isle de portraiture et de la ville des portraits," in *Voyages imaginaires, songes, visions et romans cabalistiques,* XXVI (Amsterdam: n.p., 1878), pp. 337-440. (First edition, 1659.)

19. For instance, in the *Bibliothèque françoise,* he uses the heading "Des Romans Comiques, ou Satyriques, & des Romans Burlesques." He then proceeds as if "Roman Comique" were a larger category which included the subheadings of "Satyrique" and "Burlesque." Next he speaks as if comic and satirical were two separate categories: "On parle des Romans Comiques, mais on les divise aussi en Satyriques & en Burlesques, & quelques uns sont tout cela ensemble. Les bons Romans Comiques & Satyriques semblent plûtost estre des images de l'Histoire que les autres" (BF, 57).

20. The implication in the orgy scene that death makes "reality" itself a masquerade is perhaps the only instance and the closest Sorel comes to dissolving everything.

21. Of course, Laurette and Agathe are the only exceptions in this general pattern of inefficacious disguise in the hands of the lower classes. But two factors differentiate them. First of all, they cannot be considered monomaniacs; they are mixed characters with a closer relationship to the heroes than to any other group. Second, as a lady of distinction, Agathe's disguise is used only to deceive an Englishman—a foreigner incapable of speaking French and unaware of social realities in France. There is no attempt at an indefinite change of social condition, just an episode of exploitation. Both women may be said to be in constant disguise, given the exigencies of their profession, which require youthfulness and occasionally the illusion of virginity.

## Conclusions

1. For a discussion of Sorel as an historiographer, see Orest Ranum, *Artisans of Glory,* ch. 4: "Sorel: A Novelist Turned Historiographer" (Chapel Hill: The Univ. of North Carolina Press, 1980), pp. 127-47.

## Appendix A

1. The following plot summaries are offered as a help to those who may have forgotten some of the intricate intrigues of the novels and most especially as an aid in locating episodes with minimal difficulty. They have been organized in different formats so as to reflect the different structural characters of the originals.

# BIBLIOGRAPHY

## Works by Charles Sorel Cited in the Text or Notes

Sorel, Charles. *Histoire comique de Francion*. Paris: Pierre Billaine, 1623-1626-1633. In *Romanciers du XVII<sup>e</sup> siècle*. Ed. Antoine Adam. Paris: Gallimard, 1958.

———. *Le Berger extravagant*. Paris: Toussainct du Bray, 1627.

———. *Remarques sur les XIIII livres du Berger extravagant*. Paris: Toussainct du Bray, 1628; rpt. Geneva: Slatkine, 1972.

———. *L'Anti-roman ou l'histoire du berger Lysis*. Paris: Toussainct du Bray, 1633.

———. *Polyandre, Histoire comique*. 2 vols. Paris: La Veuve Nicolas Cercy, 1648; rpt. Geneva: Slatkine, 1972-1974.

———. *La Bibliothèque françoise*. Paris: La Compagnie des Libraires du Palais, 1667; rpt. Geneva: Slatkine, 1970.

———. *De la connoissance des bons livres*. Paris: André Pralard, 1671.

———. "Description de l'isle de portraiture et de la ville des portraits" [1659]. In *Voyages imaginaires, songes, visions et romans cabalistiques*. XXVI. Amsterdam: n.p., 1878, pp. 337-400.

———. "La Louange et l'utilité des bottes." Paris: Robert Daufresne, 1622.

———. *La Maison des jeux*. 2 vols. Paris: Nicolas de Cercy, 1642.

———. *Les Nouvelles françoises*. Paris: Pierre Billaine, 1623. Rev. ed. *Les Nouvelles choisies*. 2 vols. Paris: Pierre David, 1645.

———. *Nouveau Recueil des pieces les plus agreables de ce temps*. Paris: Nicolas de Sercy, 1642.

———. *L'Orphize de Chrysante*. Paris: Toussainct du Bray, 1626.

———. *La Science universelle*. 4 vols. Paris: Toussainct Quinet, 1647-1664.

## Criticism

Alter, Jean. "La Bande à Francion ou les pièges de l'histoire." *L'Esprit Créateur*, 19 (1980), 3-13.

————. "C'est moi qui parlons: Le jeu des narrateurs dans *Francion.*" *French Forum*, 5 (1980), 99-105.

Arbour, Roméo. "Langage et société dans les *Nouvelles françoises* de Sorel." *Revue de l'Université d'Ottowa*, 41 (1971), 169-91.

Baldner, R.W. "La Jeunesse de Charles Sorel." *Dix-septième Siècle*, 40 (1958), 273-81.

Battista, Pietro. "Attualità del *Francion.*" *Le Lingue Straniere*, 14, No. 5 (September-October 1962), 14-26.

Blanzat, Jean. "Deux Romans sources." *Monde Nouveau* (January 1956), pp. 94-96.

Bugliani, Ivanna. "Francion eroe libertino." *Saggi e Ricerche di Letteratura Francese*, 7 (1966), 9-68.

Burf, Kay. "A Writer Turns against Literature: Sorel's *Le Berger extravagant.*" *Revue de l'Université d'Ottawa*, 43 (1973), 277-91.

Cazenave, Gil. "L'Image du prince dans les premiers romans de Sorel." *Dix-septième Siècle*, 105 (1974), 19-28.

Chouinard, Daniel. "Sorel (anti)romancier et le brouillage du discours." *Etudes Françaises*, 14, Nos. 1-2 (1978), 65-91.

Cristin, Claude. "Personnage méconnu, œuvre méconnue: Hortensius, Francion et Sorel." *Revue des Sciences Humaines*, 137 (1970), 5-14.

Etiemble, René. "Un Ecrivain généreux: Charles Sorel." *Hygiène des lettres*. V: "*C'est le bouquet.*" Paris: Gallimard, 1967, pp. 23-25.

Franchetti, Anna Lia. "Il *Berger extravagant* di Charles Sorel o l'inganno della rappresentazione." *Paragone*, 27, No. 318 (1976), 45-68.

————. "*Le Berger extravagant*: Analisi d'un miracolo." *Saggi e Ricerche di Letteratura Francese*, 16 (1977), 127-67.

————. Il "*Berger extravagant*" di *Charles Sorel*. Florence: Olschki, 1977.

Freudmann, Félix R. "La Recherche passionnée du *Francion.*" *Symposium*, 21 (1967), 101-17.

Garavini, Fausta. "La Casa dei giochi." *Paragone*, 26, No. 300 (1975), 3-47.

————. "*Francion* rivisitato: Diacronia d'una struttura." *Saggi e Ricerche di Letteratura Francese*, 14 (1975), 37-107.

————. "La 'Solitudine' di Sorel." *Paragone*, 28, No. 328 (1977), 60-82.

————. "L'Itinéraire de Sorel: Du *Francion* à la *Science universelle.*" *Revue d'Histoire Littéraire de la France*, 77 (1977), 432-39.

————. "L'Antiromanzo del filosofo stravagante." *Paragone*, 29, No. 340 (1978), 3-23.

Goldin, Jeanne. "Structures métaphoriques et unité narrative: Le Livre I de *L'Histoire comique de Francion.*" *Papers on French Seventeenth-Century Literature*, 4-5 (1976), 117-40.

————. "Topos et fonctionnement narratif: La maquerelle dans *L'Histoire comique de Francion.*" *Etudes Françaises*, 13, Nos. 1-2 (1977), 89-117.

Green, Frederick C. "The Critic of the 17th Century and His Attitudes toward the French Novel." *Modern Philology*, 24 (1926), 285-95.

Greenberg, Caren S. "Mediation and Madness: Charles Sorel's *Berger extravagant.*" Diss. Cornell, 1977.

Griffiths, Michael, and Wolfgang Leiner. "Some Thoughts on the Names of the Characters in Sorel's *Histoire comique de Francion.*" *Romance Notes*, 15 (1973-1974), 445-53.

Guthrie, J. Richard, Jr. "An Analysis of Style and Purpose in the First Episode of the *Histoire comique de Francion.*" *Romance Notes*, 15 (1973-1974), 99-103.

Hinterhäuser, Hans. "Qui est Francion? Préliminaire à une interprétation de l'*Histoire comique de Francion* par Charles Sorel." In *Studi in onore di Italo Siciliano*. Florence: Olschki, 1966, I, 543-56.

Judrin, Roger. "Charles Sorel." *La Nouvelle Revue Française*, 11 (1963), 291-95.

Lachèvre, Frédéric. "Pierre Louys et l'histoire littéraire: Charles Sorel et le roman *Francion.*" *Mercure de France*, 170, No. 662 (16 January 1926), 379-83.

Lefier, Yves. "Conversion ou récupération: Les trois *Francion* de Sorel, 1623-1633." *Revue de l'Université Laurentienne*, 5, No. 2 (1973), 25-34.

Leiner, Wolfgang. "Le Rêve de Francion: Considérations sur la cohésion intérieure de *L'Histoire comique.*" In *La Cohérence intérieure: Etudes sur la littérature française du XVIIᵉ siècle présentées en hommage à Judd D. Hubert*. Eds. Jacqueline Van Baelen and David L. Rubin. Paris: Jean-Michel Place, 1977, pp. 157-75.

———, et al. "Fiches signalétiques des études traitant de l'*Histoire comique de Francion* de Sorel." *Oeuvres et Critiques*, 1, No. 1 (1975-1976), 63-110.

Leroy, Jean-Pierre. "Réflexions critiques de Sorel sur son œuvre romanesque." *Dix-septième Siècle*, 105 (1974), 29-47.

Lever, Maurice. "Charles Sorel et les problèmes du roman sous Louis XIII." In *Critique et création littéraires en France au XVIIᵉ siècle*. Ed. Marc Fumaroli. Paris: Editions du C.N.R.S., 1977, pp. 18-89.

———. "Le Statut de la critique dans *Le Berger extravagant.*" *Revue d'Histoire Littéraire de la France*, 77 (1977), 417-31.

Magne, Emile. "*L'Histoire comique de Francion.*" *Mercure de France*, 186 (February 1926), 165-67.

Makiya, Cornelia Thompson. "Charles Sorel's *Polyandre, Histoire comique*: Microcosm of the *Noblesse de robe.*" Diss. Kentucky, 1974.

Mayfield, Susan Newmark. "The House of Games: The Fictional Works of Sorel." Diss. Johns Hopkins, 1975.

Minar, Jaroslav. "De *Francion* à *Gil Blas.*" *Philologica Pragensia*, 9 (1966), 264-74.

Nicolet, M. "La Condition de l'*homme de lettres* au XVII<sup>e</sup> siècle à travers l'œuvre de deux contemporains: Charles Sorel et A. Furetière." *Revue d'Histoire Littéraire de la France*, 63 (1963), 369-93.

Olivero, Adalberto. "Una Fonte inesplorata per un personnagio del *Francion*." *Studi Francesi*, 32 (1967), 280-83.

Pabst, Walter. "Funktionen des Traumes in der französischen Literatur des 17. Jahrhunderts." *Zeitschrift für Französische Sprache und Literatur*, 66 (1956), 154-74.

Ranum, Orest. *Artisans of Glory*. Ch. 4: "Sorel: A Novelist Turned Historiographer." Chapel Hill: Univ. of North Carolina Press, 1980, pp. 127-47.

Reynaud, Armand A. "Le Voyage épique de Francion." In *Travel, Quest, and Pilgrimage as a Literary Theme: Studies in Honor of Reini Virtanen*. Eds. Frans C. Amelinckx and Joyce N. Megay. Manhattan, Kansas: Society of Spanish American Studies, 1978, pp. 119-27.

Ridgely, Beverly S. "The Cosmic Voyage in Sorel's *Francion*." *Modern Philology*, 65 (1967-1968), 1-8.

Roy, Emile. *La Vie et les œuvres de Charles Sorel*. Paris: Hachette, 1891.

Serroy, Jean. "Epées et picaros." *Recherches et Travaux* (Université de Grenoble, U.E.R. de Lettres), Bull. 1 (May 1970), 15-22.

———. "D'un roman à métamorphoses: La composition du *Francion* de Sorel." *Baroque*, 6 (1973), 97-103.

———. "Francion et l'argent, ou *L'Immoraliste* et les *Faux monnayeurs*." *Dix-septième siècle*, 105 (1974), 3-18.

———. *Roman et réalité: Les histoires comiques au XVII<sup>e</sup> siècle*. Paris: Minard, 1981.

Setaro, G. "'Francion' dans la vie et dans l'œuvre de Sorel." *Revue des Langues Vivantes*, 28, No. 2 (1962), 134-48.

Skornia, H.J. "Charles Sorel as a Precursor of Realism." *PMLA*, 56 (1941), 379-94.

Sullivan, Martha Hatten. "The Structural Unity of Sorel's *Francion*." Diss. Tulane, 1969.

Suozzo, Andrew G., Jr. "Illusion and Reality in Sorel's *Francion*." Diss. Pennsylvania, 1973.

———. "Peasant Marriage and Libertine Orgy: A Note on Baroque Counterpoint in the *Francion*." *French Review*, 50 (1977), 476-79.

———. "Nays as the Vicarious Heroine: The *Francion*'s Book XII." *French Forum*, 3 (1978), 3-9.

———. "Hortensius and Collinet: Gradations and Implications of Madness in the *Francion*." *Romance Notes*, 20 (1979), 81-86.

———. "Disguise and the Rites of Death and Resurrection in Sorel's *Francion*." *French Review*, 53 (1979), 23-28.

Sutcliffe, F.C. *Le Réalisme de Charles Sorel: Problèmes humains du XVII^e siècle.* Paris: Nizet, 1965.

Thiessen, Sigrun. *Charles Sorel: Rekonstruktion einer antiklassizistischen Literaturtheorie und Studien zum "Anti-Roman."* Münchener Romantische Arbeiten, 45. Munich: Wilhelm Fink, 1977.

Tilton, Elizabeth Meier. "Concept and Technique in the Anti-Novels of Charles Sorel." Diss. Yale, 1970.

–––––. "Charles Sorel, Lawyer, and the Case of the *Berger extravagant.*" *Papers on French Seventeenth-Century Literature*, 3 (1975), 69-81.

–––––. "Structural and Linguistic Patterns in the Seventeenth-Century Novel and Anti-Novel." *Neophilologus*, 63 (1978), 212-21.

Verdier, Gabrielle-Marie. "The Art of the *Nouvelle* in Early Seventeenth-Century France: Charles Sorel." Diss. Yale, 1976.

–––––. "Tradition and 'Textuality' in a Baroque Romance: Charles Sorel's *L'Orphize de Chrysante.*" *Kentucky Romance Quarterly*, 26 (1979), 491-508.

Woodbridge, Benjamin M. "The Great and Small Infinities in Sorel." *Modern Language Notes*, 38 (1923), 442-43.

## General Criticism

Adam, Antoine. *L'Age classique.* I. Paris: B. Arthaud, 1968.

–––––. *Histoire de la littérature française au XVII^e siècle.* I. Paris: Del Duca, 1962.

Alter, Robert. *The Rogue's Progress: Studies in the Picaresque Novel.* Cambridge, Mass.: Harvard Univ. Press, 1964.

Bar, Francis. *Le Genre burlesque en France au XVII^e siècle.* Paris: D'Artey, 1960.

Barthes, Roland. *Le Degré zéro de l'écriture.* Paris: Seuil, 1953.

–––––. *S/Z.* Paris: Seuil, 1970.

Booth, Wayne C. *The Rhetoric of Fiction.* Chicago: Univ. of Chicago Press, 1961.

Cayrou, Gaston. *Le Français classique: Lexique de la langue du XVII^e siècle.* Paris: Didier, 1948.

Cerny, Vaclav. "Le Baroque et la littérature française." *Critique*, 109 (June 1956), 517; 110 (July 1956), 617-35.

Collinet, Jean-Pierre, and Jean Serroy. *Romanciers et conteurs du XVII^e siècle.* Paris: Ophrys, 1975.

Cotgrave, Randle. *A Dictionarie of the French and English Tongues.* 1611; rpt. New York: Da Capo Press; Amsterdam: Theatrum Orbis Terrarum, 1971.

Coulet, Henri. *Le Roman jusqu'à la Révolution.* Paris: Armand Colin, 1967.

Davidson, Hugh M. *Audience, Words, and Art: Studies in Seventeenth-Century French Rhetoric.* Columbus: Ohio State Univ. Press, 1965.

DeJean, Joan E. *Scarron's* Roman comique*: A Comedy of the Novel, A Novel of Comedy.* Bern: Peter Lang, 1977.

Deloffre, Frédéric. *La Nouvelle en France à l'époque classique.* Paris: Didier, 1967.

de Man, Paul. *Allegories of Reading: Figural Language in Rousseau, Nietzsche, Rilke, and Proust.* New Haven: Yale Univ. Press, 1979.

———. *Blindness and Insight: Essays in the Rhetoric of Contemporary Criticism.* New York: Oxford Univ. Press, 1971.

———. "The Rhetoric of Temporality." In *Interpretation Theory and Practice.* Ed. Charles S. Singleton. Baltimore: The Johns Hopkins Univ. Press, 1969, pp. 173-209.

Foucault, Michel. *Folie et déraison: Histoire de la folie à l'âge classique.* Paris: Plon, 1961.

Fournel, Victor. *La Littérature indépendante et les écrivains oubliés.* Paris: Didier, 1862.

France, Peter. *Rhetoric and Truth in France.* Oxford: Clarendon Press, 1972.

Frohock, W.M. "The 'Picaresque' in French before *Gil Blas.*" *Yale French Studies,* No. 38 (1967), 222-29.

Fumaroli, Marc. "Les Mémoires du XVIIe siècle au carrefour des genres en prose." *Dix-septième Siècle,* 94-95 (1971), 7-37.

Genette, Gérard. *Figures.* Paris: Seuil, 1966.

———. *Figures II.* Paris: Seuil, 1969.

———. *Figures III.* Paris: Seuil, 1972.

Green, Frederick C. *French Novelists, Manners and Ideas.* New York: D. Appleton and Co., 1931.

Le Breton, André. *Le Roman au dix-septième siècle.* 1890; rpt. Geneva: Slatkine, 1970.

Lever, Maurice. *La Fiction narrative en prose au XVIIe siècle.* Paris: Editions du C.N.R.S., 1976.

Magendie, Maurice. *Le Roman français au XVIIe siècle: De l'Astrée au Grand Cyrus.* 1932; rpt. Geneva: Slatkine, 1970.

Miller, Stuart. *The Picaresque Novel.* Cleveland: Press of Case Western Reserve University, 1967.

Morillot, Paul. *Le Roman en France depuis 1610 jusqu'à nos jours.* Paris: Masson, 1892.

Morrissette, Bruce. "Structures de sensibilité baroque dans le roman préclassique." *Cahiers de l'Association Internationale des Etudes Françaises,* 11 (1959), 86-103.

Mousnier, Roland. *Problèmes de stratification sociale*. Paris: Presses Universitaires de France, 1965.

Ratner, Moses. *Theory and Criticism of the Novel in France from L'Astrée to 1750*. New York: De Palma, 1938.

Reynier, Gustave. *Le Roman réaliste au XVII$^e$ siècle*. 1914; rpt. Geneva: Slatkine, 1971.

———. *Les Origines du roman réaliste*. 1912; rpt. Geneva: Slatkine, 1969.

Rousset, Jean. *La Littérature de l'âge baroque en France: Circé ou le paon*. Paris: Corti, 1953.

———. *Narcisse romancier: Essai sur la première personne dans le roman*. Paris: Corti, 1973.

Saussure, Ferdinand de. *Cours de linguistique générale*. Paris: Payot, 1972.

# FRENCH FORUM MONOGRAPHS

1. Karolyn Waterson. *Molière et l'autorité: Structures sociales, structures comiques.* 1976.
2. Donna Kuizenga. *Narrative Strategies in* La Princesse de Clèves. 1976.
3. Ian J. Winter. *Montaigne's Self-Portrait and Its Influence in France, 1580-1630.* 1976.
4. Judith G. Miller. *Theater and Revolution in France since 1968.* 1977.
5. Raymond C. La Charité, ed. *O un amy! Essays on Montaigne in Honor of Donald M. Frame.* 1977.
6. Rupert T. Pickens. *The Welsh Knight: Paradoxicality in Chrétien's* Conte del Graal. 1977.
7. Carol Clark. *The Web of Metaphor: Studies in the Imagery of Montaigne's* Essais. 1978.
8. Donald Maddox. *Structure and Sacring: The Systematic Kingdom in Chrétien's* Erec et Enide. 1978.
9. Betty J. Davis. *The Storytellers in Marguerite de Navarre's* Heptaméron. 1978.
10. Laurence M. Porter. *The Renaissance of the Lyric in French Romanticism: Elegy, "Poëme" and Ode.* 1978.
11. Bruce R. Leslie. *Ronsard's Successful Epic Venture: The Epyllion.* 1979.
12. Michelle A. Freeman. *The Poetics of* Translatio Studii *and* Conjointure: Chrétien de Troyes's Cligés. 1979.
13. Robert T. Corum, Jr. *Other Worlds and Other Seas: Art and Vision in Saint-Amant's Nature Poetry.* 1979.
14. Marcel Muller. *Préfiguration et structure romanesque dans* A la recherche du temps perdu *(avec un inédit de Marcel Proust).* 1979.
15. Ross Chambers. *Meaning and Meaningfulness: Studies in the Analysis and Interpretation of Texts.* 1979.
16. Lois Oppenheim. *Intentionality and Intersubjectivity: A Phenomenological Study of Butor's* La Modification. 1980.
17. Matilda T. Bruckner. *Narrative Invention in Twelfth-Century French Romance: The Convention of Hospitality (1160-1200).* 1980.
18. Gérard Defaux. *Molière, ou les métamorphoses du comique: De la comédie morale au triomphe de la folie.* 1980.
19. Raymond C. La Charité. *Recreation, Reflection and Re-Creation: Perspectives on Rabelais's* Pantagruel. 1980.
20. Jules Brody. *Du style à la pensée: Trois études sur les* Caractères de La Bruyère. 1980.
21. Lawrence D. Kritzman. *Destruction/Découverte: Le Fonctionnement de la rhétorique dans les* Essais de Montaigne. 1980.
22. Minnette Grunmann-Gaudet and Robin F. Jones, eds. *The Nature of Medieval Narrative.* 1980.
23. J.A. Hiddleston. *Essai sur Laforgue et les* Derniers Vers *suivi de* Laforgue et Baudelaire. 1980.
24. Michael S. Koppisch. *The Dissolution of Character: Changing Perspectives in* La Bruyère's Caractères. 1981.
25. Hope H. Glidden. *The Storyteller as Humanist: The* Serées *of Guillaume Bouchet.* 1981.
26. Mary B. McKinley. *Words in a Corner: Studies in Montaigne's Latin Quotations.* 1981.

27. Donald M. Frame and Mary B. McKinley, eds. *Columbia Montaigne Conference Papers*. 1981.
28. Jean-Pierre Dens. *L'Honnête Homme et la critique du goût: Esthétique et société au XVIIe siècle*. 1981.
29. Vivian Kogan. *The Flowers of Fiction: Time and Space in Raymond Queneau's Les Fleurs bleues*. 1982.
30. Michael Issacharoff et Jean-Claude Vilquin, éds. *Sartre et la mise en signe*. 1982.
31. James W. Mileham. *The Conspiracy Novel: Structure and Metaphor in Balzac's Comédie humaine*. 1982.
32. Andrew G. Suozzo, Jr. *The Comic Novels of Charles Sorel: A Study of Structure, Characterization and Disguise*. 1982.

French Forum, Publishers, Inc.
P.O. Box 5108, Lexington, Kentucky 40505

Publishers of *French Forum*, a journal of literary criticism